Dedicat

To My Dad – Joe Hill Walton

My Dad was an avid farmer. He loved his garden. He worked a full-time job during the day but he ate dinner and was off to his garden the minute he got home from work. He labored many, many hours from early spring to late fall. Plowing, fertilizing, planting, and weeding were all necessary to develop the healthy and bountiful crop he desired. Our family spent the summers hoeing, picking, harvesting, and preparing vegetables and fruits to furnish our food pantry and freezer for the winter. Dad was a generous man, so there was always plenty to share with our family and neighbors.

At the age of 63, on a hot summer day, Dad was working in his garden. About midday, he came to the house because he was hurting. Mom called me at work, just a few minutes away from her home. I came home quickly. Dad told us he thought it was his gallbladder. But shortly after that, he passed out and died right there at home. A heart attack turned our world upside down that day.

The summer after Dad passed, I planted some corn, tomatoes, okra, cantaloupe, and beans in a small area at my house down the road from Mom. The daily weeding, fertilizing, hoeing took a lot of work. Even with all my diligence, the cutworms got my tomatoes, the deer and worms ate my corn and cantaloupes. I never really understood or appreciated his hard, continual work until my experience with a garden. He paid a high price for our family and many neighbors in our community, working his garden every year. All the treasures from his garden saved us a lot of money on grocery bills. I can testify to that now with the costs of my grocery bills.

Every spring, when the weather begins to break, I can look toward my two sons' homes and see in my spirit the gardens past, and I think of you, Dad and Mom. I still miss you both daily.

The scripture on my Dad's tombstone reads:

"A sower goes forth to sow..." (Luke 8:5)

"Thank you for the SEEDS OF TRUTH you planted in my life. Thank you both for leaving a Christian legacy, an example of hard work, and hearts that were always willing to share a helping hand when there was a need in our family, Church, and community. I pray my legacy will be as fruitful as yours. In Jesus Name, Amen."

Contents

Foreword

Peggy has forty years of mission experience and is an excellent teacher and counselor. She has served on our ministry board for eighteen years and has personally traveled to Kenya time after time to represent us and encourage those who minister at House of Love. Our Board calls her "our feet in Africa."

Peggy loves the Lord, and this is evident in her teaching, preaching, and lifestyle. She is well-grounded in the Bible, highly respected in her home church, and eager to make the Lord Jesus known. Peggy goes wherever the Lord leads and is always ready to give a witness for Him when given an opportunity. She believes that everyone who claims Jesus Christ as Savior has a calling on their life for service. Service can be at home or on foreign soil, or both. You will enjoy her book because Peggy's love for Jesus and missions is present in her writing. After reading this devotional, you will feel a tug on your heart to seriously contemplate the ministry opportunities available to you. It is never too late to answer the call of Jesus, whether individually or with a team. May the Lord use this book to help you do just that?

Jan McCray

October 17, 1935 – October 4, 2021

*Ordained evangelist/speaker and
published author*

*Served the Maasai tribe in Kenya, Africa,
for over thirty years*

*Founder of House of Love,
in the village of Leshuta, Kenya*

Introduction

Have you ever wondered what your life is all about? Why you take up space on this planet? I have, for sure! So, I asked the Lord what He wanted me to do with my life—a plan and purpose, perfect just for me! Church members were continually telling me what they thought I should be doing with my life. Sunday after Sunday, the pastor's messages of go, do, be a part, teach, lead, etc., emphasized I should be DOING something. Finally, I acknowledged that I had a purpose, a destiny to embrace, and a calling to answer, given by the Creator, but I wasn't sure what it was.

Have you ever felt that way? I married my first high school sweetheart after I graduated in May 1966. There was not a lot of time for soul-searching as a single person. Jobs were hard to come by in our little town, so I settled into staying home. I found out I was pregnant after several months. Our two sons arrived within the first four years of our marriage, so I embraced a stay-at-home-mom position.

I went to work outside our home when the boys entered school. I then became a full-time mom and full-time employee. These two occupations made for rewarding years but a lot of stress as well. At times, I felt like I wasn't making any impact for good in our society.

Frankly, I felt like I had not been the best mom or wife, either. Stress began to compound, and it finally drove me to my knees in a revival meeting held in our little United Methodist Church in 1976.

At the age of 28, I asked Jesus to come into my heart and be my Savior. Even though I had attended, joined, and served in the church my whole life, this experience at that altar was the one that changed my life's direction forever.

Years of spiritual growth, healing for our marriage, and salvation for my husband and sons brought joy, peace, and fulfillment into my life. As I grew spiritually, I became aware God had additional purposes for me, along with being a wife and mother. My prayer was "God, how can I make a difference in Your kingdom?" Thoughts, little as tiny seeds, began to grow in my heart and spirit. Maybe there was another calling and purpose to embrace.

He answered my heart's prayer one weekend as I attended a women's retreat. This yearly retreat is held explicitly for educating Christian leaders. His words came to me as Scripture during this retreat weekend: "Feed my sheep!" Not many details came with this command, but another tiny seed began to grow. Many years have come and gone since that weekend. The Seed of Truth came to me in the call as a missionary. I have had the privilege of serving and traveling for the Lord for many years.

These adventures carried me to five of the seven continents sharing the love of Jesus and His gospel message. I ministered to children, women, and men and shared in numerous hours of counseling. I did my share of painting, building benches, and other light construction jobs on many trips. This commission as a missionary is a rewarding call; I do not take it lightly. Has it always been easy? By no means. Has it been a real adventure? Yes, it has! There is nothing more rewarding than seeing someone walk out of spiritual darkness into the Light of Jesus Christ. Nothing compares to witnessing a prisoner delivered from the hands of the enemy. My call to plant the seeds of the Gospel, to sometimes water them with encouragement or the privilege of harvesting them in salvation, is my delight given by the Lord.

How about you? Where are you? Do you know the purpose for which God created you? You may be considering mission work as your Calling. Let me assure you, if you know and believe in Jesus, being on mission, for sure, is your Calling. All people, naming Christ as their Savior, are called and appointed for His kingdom service. Everyone does not have the call to be a short- or long-term missionary, but all who name Jesus Christ as Savior are called to be active in His vineyard serving. His will is for all Christians to lead people into a relationship with Jesus Christ as their Savior and Lord. The second part of His destiny for you is to help them grow spiritually and become fruitful followers of Jesus, leading more laborers into His vineyard.

One of my favorite Old Testament Scriptures is Micah 6:8: "He has told you, O man, what is good; And what does the Lord require of you except to be just, and to love [and to diligently practice] kindness (compassion), and to walk humbly with your God [setting aside any overblown sense of importance or self-righteousness]?" (Amplified Version). This Scripture does not tell

you how you will fulfill your purpose or Calling, but it
does inform us about what it takes to please God. Isn't
that what we want, to please God? What a tragedy it is
to see a life God created wasted on selfish interests.

A Lot to Learn

I have made mistakes over the years on international mission trips. At times I went unprepared, with
a lack of knowledge, but not because of disobedience.
Being unprepared because you did not study or get
informed about the people and places you are going
can harm you, your team, and possibly complicate God's
purposes and plans. It could bruise the fruit God is trying to harvest through you.

Welcome to My World

A significant portion of the following devotions
contains excerpts of my testimony, things happening
before a trip, on the trip, or after returning home. I
desire to equip you to be prepared mentally, emotionally, physically, and spiritually for God's appointments.
Whether you minister abroad or home, you will find
some great Seeds of Truth herein to help you be faithful and become fruitful. Several devotionals are personal testimonies of dear friends or fellow missionaries
of mine. All contain personal knowledge and wisdom
gained through experiences in our walk with God. Most
will help you prepare for your mission by increasing
your faith in a big God who accomplishes big things in
the Spirit and physical world. There will be highlights
from home missions that are close to God's heart, as
well. Remember, I remarked earlier, all of God's children
are to be mission-minded for Him, at home and abroad.

There is always a *mission* close at hand, opportunities to give an account for the *"Hope that lies within you."* (I Peter 3:15)

Another purpose of this book is to help introduce His Calling to you and grow you in spirit so you will be ready for all you will encounter. Whether your mission is down the street or deep in African bush, all opportunities need His wisdom, extensive training, planning, listening, and much prayer. Following each devotion, you will find questions to answer, statements to ponder, and sometimes short prayers to pray to the Lord. If you allow the Holy Spirit to dig deep and plant a "Seed of Truth" in your heart, He will bring a harvest of wisdom, knowledge, and much fruit through the missions lying before you.

Clarifying Definitions

Below are some definitions, which will hopefully clarify and enlighten your understanding of this book.

Legacy: Anything handed down from the past, family, or a predecessor. Something that can be transmitted by or received from someone who has passed. Even science and history can leave a legacy.

Call, Calling, and Destiny: These three words are very similar in meaning. They denote the entwined sense of who you will be when you walk with God. When God changed Abram's and Sara's name to include letters from His name, their *Calling* and *Destiny* came to life. The appointment of a prophet, which we see in the life of Isaiah, Jeremiah, Saul to Paul, and Simon to Peter, the Rock, implies we should walk worthy of the call He places on our lives. The Calling to become His child includes the Destiny of revealing His Sovereignty to all we come in contact with by our words, deeds, or actions. When we exercise the spiritual gifts given to us, we answer His Call on our lives. Our conversion experience becomes Calling and Destiny to reveal God to our world. Thus, we are all CALLED to a DESTINY!

Planting Your Garden

What are you cultivating in your life? What kind of seeds are you planting? The Bible says, *"We will reap what we sow; like produces like."* (Luke 19:21)

Along with discovering and embracing the destiny of your life, it will include a lot of time, work, effort, "blood, sweat, and tears." You will make mistakes; I make my share. But, you will, hopefully, enjoy the fruits of your labor and service in God's garden of life.

As you delve into these devotions, realize you are sowing seeds, hoping, trusting, and believing to reap a bountiful harvest in your spiritual life and for the Kingdom of God. Pray for a good, healthy crop!

Identifying Your Call and Destiny

"... for I know the plans that I have for you,' declares the Lord, plans for welfare and not for calamity to give you a future and a hope." Jeremiah 29:11

No matter *who* you are, this is God's destiny for you. His plan for your creation is good. The way you accomplish your Calling is as diverse as people in our world; it is unique as your fingerprints are unique.

God had been silent for many years because His people turned away from Him in sin. Before God created him in his mother's womb, God called Jeremiah and commissioned him to be a prophet to His people. (Jeremiah 1:5)

A simple definition of destiny is that God knew you even before you were born, and He has a plan for your life. It's called your future or destiny. God knew Jeremiah and placed a call on his life before he ever drew his first breath. Psalms 139 confirms this, as well. The conception and birth of John the Baptist, called to be the forerunner of Jesus, is another example. God spared Moses' life because of the call on his life to deliver his people from bondage in Egypt.

Hadassah (better known as Esther) had a call on

her life to become queen. God called her to intercede, so His chosen people could be delivered from their enemy's hand.

"Elijah was a man with a nature like ours, and he prayed earnestly that it might not rain, and it did not rain on the earth for three years and six months. And he prayed again, and the sky poured rain, and the earth produced its fruit."
(James 5:17-18)

There was nothing special about Elijah in the human sense. He believed in God and responded in obedience. As in most experiences, our Calling comes in stages. The Bible says He desires to use us to further His Kingdom. But we go to Him as a child, so it takes time to mature into our destiny.

1. Have I identified my Calling, the destiny God has ordained for me? Can I put it down on paper, i.e., time, date, words spoken to me either by the Lord or through the confirmation of a servant of His?
2. What is my vision? The Bible encourages us to write our visions down. (Habakkuk 2:2) Take time to write down my Godly dreams.
3. Have I embraced my destiny and discovered my Calling? Spend time in prayer and ask God for directions and revelations.

The First Call is Salvation— Position Yourself

I was a stay-at-home mom until our sons entered school. I then went to work at a bank. I left the banking business after a few years to become a legal secretary in a law office. After gaining several years of legal secretary experience, I chose another law firm in a bigger city for a pay increase. Many different lifestyles and temptations in this law firm were unlike any I had experienced in my small country life. This job brought experiences into our marriage and home life that didn't go along with our regular church attendance. Don and I had grown up in church, but we did not know the Lord personally and were not living for Him. We attended church, but that was about all. We both made some bad decisions during this time.

It was during this season the Lord began dealing with me. His gentle but firm wooing brought me face to face with Him at a revival one night. No, He did not tell me I would become an international missionary at that time. We had the two young sons at home, and that revelation would have been too much to comprehend. All He did was call me unto Himself. My destiny would unfold a little at a time as I sought Him and embraced His Calling.

When I share with someone for the first time, I like to ask them specific questions. I am asking the same of you as you begin these devotions. The question is, "Do you know Jesus personally?" He is the One your mission is all about. You need to have the correct answer to this question. To arrive at the final destination as you travel through this book, we have only one starting point: salvation in Jesus Christ. Yes, you can accomplish good deeds and do good works without knowing and believing in Jesus. But why would you want to do that? I have found most people who know Christ are not offended when asked this question. They, hopefully, can bear witness to the love and concern for them by the person asking.

Please listen to hear His voice and answer His call to salvation. He will begin revealing His plans for your life, a little at a time. Jesus said He came to seek and save the lost. Once you know Christ, you are in a position to receive your commission and call from Him. You may not be the next Billy Graham, but you might be his/her mom or dad! Jesus, through the power of His Holy Spirit, knows the plans He has for you.

My prayer for you is that you are secure in a personal relationship with the Lord Jesus. Before you read any further in this book, I ask you to confirm your salvation and total commitment to Jesus and His Lordship over your life. I John 5:13 says, *"I write these things to you who believe in the Name of the Son of God that you may know that you have eternal life."* You can have assurance today and know the Lord Jesus Christ lives in your heart and leads your life daily. You can move on to the questions, or if you have any doubts, please pray this prayer:

"Lord Jesus, forgive me of my sins and come into my heart. I confess you are the Son of God. I ask you to sit upon the throne of my heart, lead me, and guide me through the power of your Holy Spirit. I lay down my rights to myself and give total control of my life to you. Have your way in my life, Lord. Be the center of my life. I ask you to forgive me of all my sin. Thank you for your forgiveness. Fill me with the power of your Holy Spirit now. I confirm my salvation in you today. In the Name of Jesus, Amen."

1. Is the power of the Holy Spirit evident in my life every day?
2. If He reveals some area in my life, not under the power of the Holy Spirit, will I ask the Lord to help me deal with it today?
3. I will ask the Holy Spirit to assure me of His presence and give me an open heart to hear His Calling.

Prayer is Your Foundation

O nce we have received salvation and have the assurance of a personal relationship with Christ, the only way to maintain and grow this relationship is to talk with God, to communicate with Him. To develop any relationship requires real communication, sharing of concerns, feelings, questions, fears, and praise. It is that simple but not always that easy.

You may have been raised in a church environment that required a specific way of praying, maybe rote prayers or prayers where everyone prayed the same prayer in the same way. Or perhaps you grew up with no example of praying and have no idea how to begin. Whatever your experience, you are certainly not alone or unusual. The Webster definition of prayer is "A spiritual communion with God or an object of worship, as in supplication, thanksgiving, adoration or confession."

This definition is acceptable. There are no rules attached to this definition, other than, of course, our object of worship is always the Holy Trinity: the Father, the Son, and the Holy Spirit. You may even realistically compare your prayers to God to the way you communicate with that person(s) that you love the most. A privilege

He gives us through prayer is that we can say anything and everything to Him, and our every word is protected, safe, and secure forever and ever. Our conversations are never revealed and never used against us. And yes, God answers our prayers!

Throughout the Bible, in numerous scriptures, God tells us that He hears our prayers and answers in His timing. We know that His timing is always perfect, regardless of how painful or long our waiting may be. Psalm 37:7 reminds us, *"Be still in the presence of the Lord and wait patiently for Him to act..."* To understand your Calling, you must pray, ask and wait for God to reveal your Calling to you. I promise that He will; remember, it may be a little at a time. I have heard this saying many times: "Prayer is a discipline first, and then it becomes a desire." I can tell you now that this is true. If developing the habit of praying seems hard at first, don't worry; it is okay. That will change; keep doing it. Remember, if you want to hear from God, you must position yourself to listen. (It's important to tune out ALL influences distracting you from hearing from the Lord.) Be Still!

Peggy: The above definition of prayer is from my special friend and prayer partner, Melissa Beasley. Your call to be on mission for Christ must be bathed and soaked in prayer. Your time in prayer is when God will dress you for your battles at home and in the field. Believe me when I say, if you give the enemy an inch, he will take a mile. He will try to wreck your trip and cause disunity to develop in your home life as well. Develop a discipline to seek God through His Word and prayer every day.

1. How is my prayer time? Do I feel connected with my Heavenly Father when I pray?

2. If I want to increase my intimacy with God, I must discipline myself. Time means attention, and attention turns to intimacy when my focus is God.

3. "Lord, help me begin a discipline of prayer and time in Your Word. My walk with You, Lord, depends on it."

Two are Better than One

Don and I, over the years, have attended many couple retreats and Christian growth conferences. Every one of them has been a building stone in our walk with the Lord. We are who we are today because of these spiritual opportunities. Each of them gave us vital new Biblical truths to practice in our individual lives and our marriage. I doubt that we would be together today or maybe not even walking with the Lord if we had not sought knowledge outside the walls of our Church. Some of these opportunities continue to open doors of ministry for us today.

In almost all of these weekends of teachings and personal soul searching, the one thing present and made to be the center of Truth in our relationship and our Christian walk was prayer. On one specific weekend, early on, we were challenged to pray together as husband and wife. After we returned home, we began praying together morning and night. Learning to pray together was awkward at first. You begin to know your partner at a depth that is not possible any other way. Daily prayer times as a couple did not take away from personal time with the Lord, but it enhanced our walks and brought a depth in our marriage hard to explain.

We take turns praying; he prays on certain days, morning and night, and I pray the other days, morning and night. Since Don retired several years ago, we share a devotion in the morning and then have our prayers. There is nothing like the intimacy you can experience with your mate when you pray together daily. The Word says, *"Don't let the sun go down on your anger."* (Ephesians 4:26) If you follow this principle, it will enrich your marriage, walk with the Lord, and help solve many anger issues.

How vital is prayer to you? I will tell you quickly that if you are seeking God for your Calling, purpose, or destiny, you will not be in the position to hear from God without spending personal time in prayer. Remember: prayer is a discipline first, and then it becomes a desire. If you want to hear from God, you must position yourself to listen. And, as my friend Melissa says, tune out ALL influences taking your attention away from hearing from the Lord; this means no cell phones or ringing phones in proximity to your place of prayer.

We have two small dogs. They always want to be where we are. Over several prayer times, we trained them to sit or lie quietly and listen to us pray. At the end of our prayers, we close the same way every time; when they hear Ephesians 3:21 and the final words, "generations forever and ever! Amen," they jump down and start dancing around wanting their treat. Indeed, if we can train our dogs to sit quietly in prayer, you can experience the presence of God through your time alone with Him.

1. How would I rate my discipline in prayer and study time of God's Word?
2. Read Ecclesiastes 4. What do these Scriptures mean if I would use them in the context of prayer?
3. Am I willing to share prayer time with my spouse or a friend? Do I believe this would benefit my walk with the Lord?

My Call from God
Through His Willing Vessels

The gentleman had squandered his younger life on substance abuse before coming to know the Lord, maybe in his sixties. Because of a terrible tractor accident, he prayed a desperate prayer, "God save me, and I will serve you the rest of my life!" God heard his prayer and miraculously saved and healed him. God then set him and his wife on a course of mission work in Mexico for their remaining years. By the end of their lives, they had built hundreds of churches and a Bible school and ministered the love of Jesus to thousands. Age should never be a factor in the fulfillment of your destiny.

Our Church began building churches in 1979 under the leadership of this elderly missionary couple. They had lived in Mexico for many years, serving diligently in ministry and meeting people's needs. Both had a heart of compassion and love for the people. At the time of our meeting, they had moved back to live in the U.S. and host teams traveling back and forth to Mexico.

My first trip was in February of 1980, the year missions stole my heart! If I am at home for a while, my heart begins to burn with a yearning "to go"! I will never forget some words they shared, "You can feed the hungry, who you will always have with you, but the most important thing you can do is share Jesus." I will forever be in debt to this couple for sharing their lives, love for Jesus and fellow man.

I am no "spring chicken." I am 72 years young; we have been married for 54 years with two married sons and daughters-in-love, who have blessed us with five grown grandchildren. We also have a great-grandson who turned three in April, 2021.The light of our old age!

I grew up in the Church and became a member but did not accept the Lord until I was 28 years old. Yes, I served in many capacities but had not made a personal commitment to Christ. You don't become a Christian by attending Church, serving, or because your parents are Christians. You become a Christian only by making a personal decision to accept Christ. God doesn't have grandchildren.

When my Dad passed away suddenly in 1991, I was 42 years old. The death of a loved one can have a way of "focusing your destiny." During my grief, I prayed Dad's legacy would become fruitful in my life. Dad loved people and had a servant's heart. He was active and supportive of the mission work in Mexico. I, too, want to leave a Godly legacy.

The Lord has called me "to go into the entire world and preach the gospel." He set that course in motion on my first mission trip to Mexico. Over the years, He has clarified His "destiny call" upon my life and fine-tuned it in many ways. I have answered this call since 1980.

I have had the privilege for the last 40 years to travel to five continents and minister in various ways in the Name of Christ. The Lord spoke to me several years ago through His Word and said, *"My latter days would be greater than my former days."* (Haggai 2:9) I have seen this come to pass. I am a blessed daughter of God.

A popular contemporary song says, "I want to leave a legacy, how will they remember me?" After listening to this song many times, I realize the legacy I want to leave is pointing to "Jesus," not me. When I have passed, I want my family to say, "She wasn't perfect for sure, but she loved Jesus, and she loved us." All of my mission work will have been in vain if they say anything else.

My prayer for you is that you seek God while there is time. He will reveal your Calling and destiny for your life, *"For He knows the plans He has for you…"* (Jeremiah 29:11)

1. How about me? Do I just exist, go through the motions, or do I know my destiny? What is my purpose and calling on my life at this moment?
2. Spend some quiet time with the Lord. What would I like for my epitaph to be when I pass from this life? Am I fulfilling my purpose? Does my life have meaning?

"Behold He makes all things new..." Isaiah 43:18

God is always creating new beginnings. We can trust Him; we love new phases of His work in our life. I love the end of a year and the beginning of a new year. It is like sunrises and sunsets. They indicate new beginnings to me; it is like our awesome God to end the old and make everything unique every day.

At my age, time is of the essence; I realize I have lived three-fourths of my life. Not being morbid here, just stating facts. God has kept His Word He promised several years ago, "...my latter years would be greater than my former years." I am walking in this promise and will continue until I draw my last breath, hopefully.

On one of my first trips to Kenya, as I was seated in a little mud-dung house, with only the light of the fire in the middle of the room, I heard the Lord speak to me about writing a book on missions. I chuckled to myself since English was not one of my best subjects in school. Actually, basketball was my best subject. I do love writing, especially about all the mission opportunities He has given to me. I love blazing trails and new adventures. I will continue going as long as He calls and equips me.

During several trips with different ministries, the missionaries began to speak to me about becoming an ordained member of the clergy. Frankly, I was polite and listened but I didn't think God had that in store for me— it certainly wasn't on my radar! I was satisfied with being a missionary and serving in the Kingdom. I knew God had called me to international missions; that was good enough for me. I have to be honest here and say I had heard Him speak about ordination before but quickly rebuked the Devil, thinking it was he and not God. I listened but then dismissed the thoughts and the recommendations. The Lord continued to speak through His servants to me about ordination.

Finally, one of the mission couples I often travel with spoke seriously to me about ordination. The gentleman sponsored me to the mission organization board he serves on, and this mission board ordained me in 2010. I know it is only because of God's anointing I can ever be of service in His Kingdom. He will use any willing vessel, even me, such as I am, a cracked pot!

1. How about me; is God calling me into full-time ministry for Him? (Let me answer that question for you: "Yes, you are commanded into full-time ministry because all who love Jesus have a call on their life. Sometimes we are not a paid servant/worker, but the lasting benefits and rewards are certainly out of this world. Take time to ponder your call.")

2. Am I willing to ask, listen, hear, and respond in faith to His call on my life? It may be in my community and not internationally. Then again, it

may be to the uttermost parts of the world. I will never know until I ask and wait for Him to tell me and give me direction.

3. I need to spend some serious time with the Lord and allow Him to open my spiritual ears to hear Him speaking to me.

A Prodigal Son Returns Home

"Welcome Home!"

*"Discipline and correction make one wise,
but a child left to himself brings disgrace and shame
to his parents." Proverbs 29:15*

My name is Ron Dupree, and this is my testimony.

This verse of Scripture sums up my childhood, teenage years, and my twenties. After around ten years of age, living in downtown Atlanta, Georgia, there were no parental boundaries. I did what I felt like doing.

The self-serving stronghold this created shone its ugly face in every area of my existence for 20+ years. Of course, the abundance of corrupt seeds sown produced many (not so pretty) crops that I would harvest. A wild ride, to say the least.

At 33 years old, I had burned through every relationship and found myself homeless, penniless, with no car, and nowhere to turn. I had not talked to any of my family for 6 or 7 years. I had hit "bottom."

Then, out of nowhere, my Grandmother's sister found me. She took me to her home, and we talked about Jesus Christ. She made a straightforward statement,

"Best I see it, Jesus is God."

That night I prayed, "Jesus, if you are real and you are God, take me, change me; I can't go on this way any longer." I saw a vision in my mind's eye of Him reaching out and taking me in His arms and holding me.

When I awoke the next morning, I knew I was a different man. The burden was gone. I felt hope and an overwhelming sense of love. The date: January 12, 1983.

Six weeks after I was born-again, in 1983, I was in a motor home with 12 other people headed to Mexico to help the young people at a seminary in Monterrey, Mexico. The Truth is, I didn't help them very much, quite the opposite. Those teenagers were on fire for the Gospel, and it radiated from them in their actions, their words, their entire being. It was contagious. I realized on the way home; the trip was not about them being "helped;" it was God's gift to me. Being around those kids lit a flame in my belly that changed my life.

Subsequently, over the following year, God allowed me the honor of seeing many hurting people come to Christ, transformed in an instant. It was a thrilling journey to travel to several countries, such as Mexico, Columbia, Peru, Ghana, and Nigeria. I also visited many states in the U.S., and, as I shared the Gospel, I found it to be real and powerful. The good news of the Gospel changes all seeking, hungry, and hurting, regardless of the language barrier or geography.

God never blesses "one-sided"—there is always mutuality when He's in the deal. We go to help; we get helped. We go to bless; we get blessed. We go to give, and we receive.

"Many are called, few are chosen." We are all called.

The chosen are the ones that are "willing." God's Love and Favor have manifested in a gazillion different ways since that day, 37 years ago. The spiritual and material blessings have been more abundant than seem possible. But that's God and how He works (if we let Him).

Peggy: I have known Ron for many years. His stepmom was my aunt, my Mom's sister. She married Ron's dad after his Mom passed away from cancer. Fate and the Lord brought her to marry Ron's Dad after her husband had died of tuberculosis. Sadly, Ron's Dad died in a tragic car accident on November 17, 1976. After Ron came to the Lord, he reunited with his stepmom and two half-brothers. Ron loved and respected his stepmom until her death. He also has a great relationship now with his two step-brothers and their family. God is still in the business of changing ashes to beauty!

When I asked Ron to share his testimony, he willingly agreed. He had no knowledge of the content and structure of my book. God affirmed to me my content and structure after receiving his testimony. We all have a Calling to honor and serve our Living God. He is the Redeemer of all things in our life.

1. Have I ever been the prodigal? Read Luke 15:11-32.
2. Who do I identify with the most, the son who went away or the son who stayed home?
3. Have I discovered the power of the Gospel?
4. Would I be able to present the Gospel on a mission trip to someone that had never heard of Jesus?

Seed of Truth #8

Free to Serve

Are you free?

A lot of people have died in our country so you and I can be free: free to worship; free to burn the U.S. flag; free to spit on the Holy Bible; freedom to pursue life, liberty, and the pursuit of happiness; and free to speak anyway we would like, good or bad, about Jesus. I am thankful for the freedoms I have and enjoy. When I began this article, I was sitting in one of my most favorite places surrounded by trees, birds chirping, and deer eating the blackberries in my view. I was enjoying the quietness of no traffic and no lights to keep me awake at night. Early in the morning, I watched the 6:30 a.m. sunrise come over the mountains from the porch. What a beautiful sight it was!

I have traveled to many places, but no place compares to home and the blessings we enjoy here. Will we continue to have these blessings from God? Only He knows the heartbeat of our nation. Only He knows what our future holds. His Word says, *He will bless those that bless Israel, and He will curse those who do not.* (Genesis 12:3) I hope and pray; you will join me to pray for our nation and Israel. God help us if we do not. I am proud to be an American, even though we have significant flaws and issues.

There is a contemporary song whose words are as follows: "You never know why you are alive until you know what you would die for." ("Live Like We're Dying" by Kris Allen)

Are you free today? Does the enemy of your soul have a hold on you? Have you moved your ancient borders and allowed him to put you in bondage or steal your freedom? The longer you stay out of God's will, the quicker the enemy can bring you down. On the mission field, the enemy will know if you are in Christ or just along for the ride and experience. We cannot fool him. Be free in Jesus; give no opportunity to the enemy. If you give him a break, he will crush you, your family and destroy your hope in Christ. He will also whip you on the mission field.

More precious to me than my American freedom is the freedom I have in Christ. Freedom to follow Jesus and be a part of His kingdom. Do you have that freedom today? Does the enemy quiver when you get out of bed in the morning? Are you dressed for battle? There is a war raging against the enemy you will meet before, on, and after this trip?

1. What is the most precious freedom I am experiencing at this time? Why do I consider it the most precious one?
2. If I travel outside the U.S., will I notice many social differences and religious traditions? How do I hope to respond to these differences?

3. "Lord, will you help me prepare for the situations I will encounter on this upcoming trip? What changes do I need to make to prepare, Lord?"

The Importance of Mentors in the Faith

You do not have to rub shoulders with someone very long to know their hearts and spirits or come to love them as a brother in Christ. Don and I began attending West Ridge in 2002. It is a megachurch with over 4,000 attendees. I always said, I didn't want to attend a church where I didn't know everybody. You know how that goes—never say never!

From the minute we walked in the door that first Sunday, we felt at home. The atmosphere was alive with passion expressed through the people who welcomed us, the people on the stage, the music, from every area of our experience. We did know several families attending this Church, and they had highly recommended it to us. We were drawn in with just one visit. We would make this our new church home.

Our pastor, Brian Bloye, and the leadership team began the Church with a small number of couples in 1997. Due to his leadership and God's blessings, the Church quickly grew into thousands in five years. With this type of growth, Pastor Brian had invited his Dad, John Bloye, a pastor, to come to join the staff.

At that time, I was in the process of obtaining my degree in Christian counseling. I made an appointment with Pastor John to discuss the counseling program at our Church. Pastor John came on staff as our Pastor of Care. It was a perfect title for him; he truly loved people, all people, and everyone loved him. His personality was infectious, and his service and love for Jesus radiated from his person. Our meeting went well and he told me to contact him when I had obtained my degree. During this meeting, we talked about missions, as well. I learned then how much Pastor John loved serving on mission trips.

Pastor John won my heart immediately with his love for missions, at home as well as foreign. Shortly after he came on staff at West Ridge, we began our Church building program. We would soon have our facilities and would not be meeting in the school anymore. He was there to participate in our groundbreaking ceremonies for our building. We were all excited about this venture.

I learned a lot from Pastor John, affectionately called Papa John, by those who knew him well. Don and I were involved with him and Judy, his wife, in a small group for a season. He exhibited the spiritual fruit of being an entirely devoted follower of Jesus, and his personality was magnetic to draw you to the Lord.

1. Do I have a "Pastor John" in my life, someone I look up to as an example of Christ?
2. Have I been that example or mentor to someone in their walk with Jesus?
3. How do I think this mission trip will affect my witness to those who look up to me?

Honorary Mention of Mentors

There are four friends and mentors who are noteworthy of honorary mention because their impact was instrumental in shaping my vision and Calling.

I have traveled with them at least once or more on a foreign trip and have experienced community service with them. Their teachings and Godly advice about serving the Lord have been vital in my Christian walk. These men live their lives in service for the Lord Jesus Christ without compromise and with the anointing of the Holy Spirit. Their prayers for me and the ministry that God has given to me have been priceless.

Mark Nysewander

Mark Nysewander is a former pastor of mine and a spiritual father to me. Mark has been a pastor, teacher, missionary, and evangelist. He authored four books; the most recent is *Revival Rising*. Mark now serves as pastor at Church on the Hill in Dalton, Georgia. He and his wife Kathy have three children and six grandchildren.

Brian Bloye

Brian planted West Ridge Church in Northwest Atlanta in 1997. Since then, West Ridge has helped to plant 185 churches in the U.S. and other churches internationally. Brian launched Engage Churches in 2015, a ministry designed to encourage, equip, and connect church planting couples. He and his wife Amy co-authored the book, *It's Personal: Surviving and Thriving on the Journey of Church Planting*. Brian is the President and co-founder of Engage Burkina, an organization devoted to reaching the people of Burkina Faso, Africa, by planting churches, providing clean water, improving education, and helping the physically disabled.

Craig Parson

Craig is an ordained member of the clergy. In 1995, he and his wife Becky founded a ministry known as Living Water Ministries—now known as the Warehouse of Hope since 1997—located in Metro Atlanta, Georgia. This ministry meets the physical and spiritual needs of people in their community and surrounding counties. Craig and Peggy, along with a team, have shared several mission trips to Nigeria. Peggy served as a volunteer as well as staff for Warehouse of Hope in the past.

Paul and Karen Whitley

Paul and Karen Whitley are ordained members of the clergy and founders of Invading the Darkness. For nearly 30 years, they have come alongside international pastors and leaders exhorting, encouraging, training, and equipping them through conferences, seminars, and acts of service. They are also instrumental in raising awareness for missions by hosting mission teams to different places internationally. Paul also serves as Chairman of Missions for Faith Christian Fellowship International, a mission society organization located in Richmond, Indiana. The Whitleys reside west of Atlanta, Georgia.

The Fellowship of the Unashamed

Testimony by Diane Bottcher

Our mission team searched our souls as we shared the first night; we entered Cuba. In the morning, we would be meeting with the people we had planned to minister to and share the love of Christ. We wanted our hearts and our hands prepared for our mission; so, that night, my precious mentor, Pastor John Bloye, and

I adopted this prayer of commitment from an unknown author. We personalized this prayer and adapted it for our trip and ourselves:

"I am part of the fellowship of the unashamed. I have Holy Spirit power; the die has been cast. I have stepped over the line. The decision has been made; I am a disciple of His. I will not look back, let up, slow down, back away, or be still.

My past has been redeemed, my present makes sense, and my future is secure. I am finished and down with low living, sight walking, small planning, smooth knees, colorless dreams, tamed visions, mundane talking, cheap giving, and dwarfed goals.

I no longer need preeminence, prosperity, position, promotions, plaudits, or popularity. I don't have to be right: first, tops, recognized, praised, regarded, or rewarded. I now live by faith, lean on His presence, walk by patience, lift by prayer, and labor by power.

My face is set, my gait is fast, my goal is heaven, my road is narrow, my way is rough, my companions are few, my Guide is reliable, my mission is clear. I cannot be bought, compromised, detoured, lured away, turned back, deluded, or delayed.

I will not flinch in the face of sacrifice, hesitate in the presence of adversity, negotiate at the table of the enemy, ponder at the pool of popularity, or meander in the maze of mediocrity.

I will not give up, shut up, let up until I have stayed up, stored up, prayed up, paid up, and preached up for the cause of Christ. I am a disciple of Jesus. I must go until He comes, give until I drop, preach until all know, and work until He stops me—my banner of identification with Jesus will be clear. So, be it, amen." ("Fellowship of the Unashamed: A Martyr's Prayer" by Clayton Kraby[1])

As we met with the sister church locals in Cotorro all week, they exhibited what Pastor John always exhibited: they were a people God-struck. They were a congregation that stood, moved, served, worked, and persevered in awe and service to our King. Their love for Him was contagious!

These people, living under Communism and in poverty, have the Holy Spirits power evidenced in their lives. They never backed down, let up, or slowed down. Their faces were set, their gait was fast, their goal was heaven, their Guide was reliable, their mission was clear. They did not flinch in the face of sacrifice or hesitate in all the adversity they daily experience. They were true disciples of Jesus. Their commitment is to serve until He comes, give until they drop, preach until all know, and work until He calls them home. Because they understand Who their Banner is. They are God-struck.

They bow in awe of the King, humbled in His Presence. I want to be that way. How is it that when I go on a mission trip, thinking I can make some impact, *I* am the one who returns home significantly impacted, knowing I received more than I could ever have given?

Peggy: I met Diane Bottcher for the first time when our Church was organizing our first trip to Cuba. We became close friends. We had a wonderful, successful trip to Cuba. I have been in a women's Bible study group that meets at her home for many years. Diane almost made a trip to Russia with our team but had to drop

---

1   Available at https://reasonabletheology.org/fellowship-of-the-unashamed-a-martyrs-prayer/

due to important issues. Not many things can draw you together to create lasting bonds like missions. Diane has seen me through some hardships, and supports me with her love, friendship and finances. We adopted that mantra then and haven't changed our minds at all!

1. Can I adopt this mantra for myself? Am I this committed to the cause of Christ?
2. Seek the Lord; ask Him to set my heart like flint. Discuss this commitment with those close to me and my team.

Seed of Truth #11
(Utah)

"Study to show yourself approved."
2 Timothy 2:15

Diane Bottcher and I had the privilege of making one other trip with Papa John. Our Church organized a mission trip to Utah. West Ridge had planted a church there, and we went to canvas the area and invite people to the new Church. Our trip would be at the very end of the year, and we would share New Year's Day with our church plant and guests attending.

We visited door to door in numerous subdivisions in the area near the Church. In this area, it is predominately one denomination. We met many parishioners from their movement on our visits. They listened as we shared with them about the new church opening. Most were cordial but had little to say to us.

At the end of each visit, we would ask if there were any prayer requests to take back to our team. At one house, the lady was cordial as we shared with her about the new Church. When we started to leave, we asked if she had any prayer requests; she hesitated and then began to share her child was dealing with some kidney issues. My partner asked if we could pray personally with the child, and this shut the mom down. We apologized profusely for asking and promised to take the request back to our team for prayer. We learned a few things on this trip. A study of dos and don'ts about the community to which you are visiting is vitally important.

Our church plant is now thriving and doing well. I pray that the child's kidney issue was resolved and not life-threatening.

Before I go on a trip now, I become aware of the location and the people who live there. It is always important to become knowledgeable of any different beliefs and religions in the area. It is a good habit that might save some embarrassment for you and the team.

On our free day of this trip, some teams went snowmobiling, and some went skiing. Since I had never had these soft-ball knees on a pair of skis, I chose snowmobiling with Diane and Pastor John. They both had experience in this sport. There were many feet of snow on the ground. We started our excursion following the trail we were to take. There were snow barriers on the sides of the path. If you got off the course, bad news, you would sink and bury your snowmobile. We were laughing and having a great ride until I ran off the trail and banked my snowmobile. Pastor John helped me back on the bike and the track, and off we went. I thought I was getting the hang of it, but I banked again and then a third time. After the third time, Papa John said to me, "Come on, Peggy, you just ride with me!" I don't think I was born for that sport. We had a lot of great laughs about it, though!

1. Do I have a spirit of discernment that will benefit me on the trip?

2. Am I willing to learn all I need to know before this trip? Am I flexible enough to be stretched?

3. Am I open spiritually to learn from those that know more than I do?

4. "Lord, please give me a friend who is committed to You and can be a spiritual mentor for me. To serve You is my greatest blessing. I also know that there can be many shared, happy memories from a trip for me. A deep trusting relationship, I believe, will enrich my walk with You."

Seed of Truth #12
(Cuba)

Ministry in a Communist Country

It was June 2004, and our Church was planning a mission trip to Cuba. Pastor John Bloye was the pastor/leader for the trip. Our team began meeting, planning, and sharing our walks as we organized our trip. The day of our trip arrived, and with much anticipation, our team was off to Cuba, a Communist country.

Upon arrival at our hotel, we discussed our plans

for the next day and our meeting time for the following day. As our team leader, Papa John discussed the agenda details and asked if anyone needed a wake-up call for the next morning. In passing, he commented, "I have an internal clock." So, he was sure he would wake up. We closed out the day with devotions and prayer and were off to bed. It had been a busy traveling day.

At the appointed meeting time the next morning, our team gathered on the bus. We waited and we waited but no John! Finally, Papa John appeared and hustled aboard the bus; he informed us his internal clock had failed him that morning! One of the many things I loved about him was his ability to laugh at himself. Yes, he could be serious when needed, but he could be so much fun, as well.

Another incident that had us all laughing was on one morning when Papa John tried to come down the stairs instead of the elevator. He could not find a door unlocked to open into a hallway. He had been calling and knocking on the doors, but no one could hear him. Finally, someone came to his rescue and opened the door for him. Once again, we laughed together and made another trip memory.

Our days were busy with Vacation Bible School for the children, visiting in the communities, women's ministry, and anything else the Lord brought across our paths. In the evening, we held services at the Church, and Papa John would preach. He was an anointed man.

I remember one specific message when he shared a desire of his heart and spirit for years, which was to preach in a communist country. He also commented with passion, "Lord, I am now ready to come home." I will never forget it.

As our team would gather on the bus each morning, Papa John would share a few thoughts for the day, and we would have a prayer. One morning during this time, he looked about the bus seriously and intently at each of us, and said, "I would gladly give my life for any of you." It is a memorable moment etched in my memory. It was almost as if Jesus stood before us speaking these words. Pastor John and his character caused our team to bond in friendship in such a short time. Missions will do that to you! You will make close friends for life.

Our trip ended, and we returned home. This trip was an experience none of us in attendance would ever forget.

1. Who are the dedicated Christians that have made impressions of Christ in my life? Who is my Papa John?
2. Do I exhibit similar impressions to people I know and influence daily? Am I ready and willing for the Lord to use my witness in this way?
3. Do I think being a devoted follower of Christ is fulfilling? What Christian attributes will I bring to the table on a trip I may take?

Privilege and Responsibility

*"Some costs accompany the privilege
of going in His Name."*

My first several years of mission ministry were in Mexico. Our Church had the connections because our former pastor had gone on staff at the Seminary there in Monterrey, Mexico. We made one to three trips a year to do different types of ministry and construction.

We traveled by plane on our first few trips but, thereafter, we would rent a large recreational vehicle and drive. By the time we reached our destination, our team would bond in spirit through our praying and singing the thousands of miles we had traveled. Along the way, we shared Jesus and saw people come to the Lord, prayed with sick people, and handed out Christian tracts all across the states. We felt we could quench the fires of hell with a water pistol.

What you will experience with a team could be life-changing for you. Some of the experiences may radically change your theology and spiritual temperament. I used to explain what happened on the trips and the things I experienced; people would look at me like I was from another world. Some things lose their meaning in translation.

This mission trip may bring changes in your life that might cost you something precious. You must be ready to pay that price for growth and change.

1. Am I willing for people to call me a fanatical Christian? (My definition of a fanatic is "someone who loves Jesus more than the person calling you a fanatic.")
2. Am I willing to sacrifice a few good things for the best Christ has to offer to me?
3. What changes would I like to take place in my life because of this trip?

Seed of Truth #14

Ready for Change

"There will be change, hopefully for good."
Russia: Sometimes ministry changes; be ready, be flexible!

Ihave been on many mission trips; each one was different: different churches, ages of people, and various ministries to be performed. I had the privilege of being a part of miraculous physical healings and spiritual healings. I had the opportunity of praying with people to accept the Lord and spur them on to grow in their walk with the Lord. I prayed with couples for the restoration of their marriage and with parents with wayward children. I can honestly say I have never been on a trip when team members I was traveling with came home personally the same way they left the states. I experience change on every journey I make for the Lord.

I had the privilege to travel to five continents in the past 40 years. My latter days are better than my former days. My life is continually changing. Most changes are due to what I have experienced and what I have seen worldwide on mission trips.

I love to travel with people on their first mission trip. I have seen God radically change who they were because of the trip. I have seen team members come to the Lord once they realized they were out of their comfort zone; their faith was not in Christ but their capabilities. Your faith increases when you know you must depend on the Lord only.

When you travel internationally to some of the poorest places in our world, you realize how blessed you are to enjoy the conveniences you have here in the U.S. When you return home, you will appreciate the running warm water, electricity, warm home during the cold months, and cooling conveniences during the hot months, being able to buy a hamburger or an ice cream if you choose. You are stretched on the mission field when inconvenienced for the Gospel's sake. It can change your life and outlook forever.

1. Am I ready for a change? Does my faith need to be challenged for spiritual growth?
2. How might this trip change me?
3. I will write down what is on my heart about this trip and possible changes that might take place in my life.
4. I will ask the Lord what changes He wants me to make.

God is Sovereign

"God watches over us, a testimony to His Sovereignty."

Don and I had returned from a cruise. We were driving home from Florida, and we made a stop. As Don got out of the car, he looked down at the left front tire. (Which he said was unusual for him to do.) The tire had split in a worn area.

Immediately, we realized the miracle of protection under which we had been driving for two hours or more. Our van is a front-wheel-drive vehicle. If that tire had blown while traveling 70 or 75 miles per hour, only the Lord knows what would have happened. As grace would have it, right across the street from where we stopped was a Ford/Chevrolet dealership. We drove over and talked to the service manager. He made a call and pointed us in the direction of a service station right down the road that sold tires. We drove to this station, and they replaced all four tires. Within an hour, we were back on the road.

What makes this story even more interesting is that Mom and I had just returned from Florida several weeks before this incident. We had rented a vehicle to drive to Lakeland to visit a friend. Don was concerned we might have trouble with my van. He wanted us to rent a newer model vehicle to make our trip. If we had driven my van, the tire incident would have happened to Mom and me on the road. I would have been in the position to handle the tire incident myself.

On the other hand, there was the possibility of a blowout on the expressway. Lord only knows how I would have handled a blowout. I cringe to think what could have happened.

Is God good or what? How many times a day does He save us from an incident or an accident? His grace covers us consistently. I thank Him for His covering of protection, love, mercy, and grace. He watches over us all, even those that do not acknowledge His protection; "He holds the whole world in His hands," as the song says. Nothing happens to anyone that does not come across His desk first. He is the Sovereign God of the Universe. I love Him and thank Him daily for His protection over our family and us.

1. Do I believe in the Sovereignty of God? Does this attribute of God give me peace and assurance for this trip and my everyday life?
2. Ponder an incident in which I physically or emotionally was ministered to by the Sovereign God of the universe.
3. Has there been a time in which I questioned God's Sovereignty? Does this incident still bother me? Today is the day to resolve that issue.

Being an Instrument of God
Is the Blessing

"We are to make Disciples for Jesus;
we are to lead for Christ."

It took me five years to feel secure enough with my connections to go to India to minister. For years, I had dreamed of India and doing mission work there. I met an Indian pastor/dean of a seminary outside Mumbai, India. He stayed in our home several times, and we communicated often. He kept saying, "Peggy, come and teach in the seminary." Finally, I decided to plan a trip. I felt God's timing was right.

I began putting the word out I was going to India. I planned to take only two or three people on a team. One thing led to another, and I had two people wanting to make the trip with me, one from New York, and another person from Georgia.

Shortly after I began to plan the trip, I embraced another leg on the trip. This request came through a dear friend of mine who has an international women's ministry connection in an area deep in the middle of India. This lady was on my friend's ministry team. I brought her on as the third person to join my team. We would be spending time with a family who had founded a children's home. We would also have speaking engagements in and around their city. The total length of our trip would be three weeks.

As the time approached for our journey, for one reason or another, the team dropped down to the one person from New York. Little did I know what the Lord had in store for us two. We often communicated before our trip. We would meet each other face to face the first time when we arrived in Mumbai, India. She flew in from New York, and I flew in from Georgia.

When I met my traveling partner there at the airport, we became immediate sisters in the Lord. As we began our journey, she shared with me how she, for many years, had felt God was calling her to minister in India. We have a mutual friend who had forwarded my monthly newsletter to her, inviting anyone interested in making the trip with me; this was how we became connected for the journey.

We had a phenomenal three weeks of ministry from Mumbai, down to Coimbatore, east coast, and west coast, even down to India's tip—a trip of a lifetime that I will never forget.

You never know what God may do when you plan a mission trip or participate in one scheduled through another party. God may use you to introduce the next C. T. Studd or Amy Carmichael or even Mother Theresa to their destiny ordained by God.

1. How did the Lord speak to me about this mission? Did He use someone else to help me along with my decisions?

2. Do I think God can supernaturally use me to be the calling agent for someone else?
3. Am I ready for God to use me; is this what discipleship is all about?

Seed of Truth #17
(India)

Birthing a Missionary

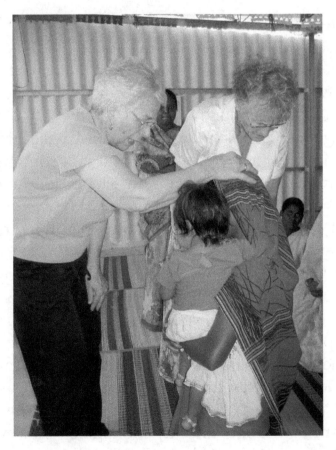

As I shared previously, Bonnie and I met in Mumbai, India, around midnight. We were both exhausted but very excited about finally meeting face to face. It seemed as if we already knew each other after all our correspondence about the trip.

Bonnie is a dear sister in the Lord to me. Who knows if I will ever see her in person again this side of Heaven? She has been so encouraging to me over the last few years. I asked her to share her testimony with me to encourage you with what God did in her life regarding missions.

Bonnie's Testimony

God called me into the missionary ministry at age 65; this was something I had never thought about or never was on my heart. I did not want to leave the country, fly, or go to a country where I could not understand the language. Therefore, I gave the Lord a hard time initially but finally agreed to pray about it. It soon became my passion. I knew from the start where He wanted me to go. I found myself crying out to God to send me to India. I cannot put into words how I felt in my heart. I just knew!

I had no idea how to arrange a mission trip, and our Church had not sent anyone in over 20 years. I had no resources or help. I looked in Christian magazines, asked people from other churches, and no one could help me. Most organizations wanted long-term missionaries. God assured me I would know when it was time.

I went to a Christian Camp in Findley, New York, for a work weekend, and my roommate was a woman from Fredonia, New York. I shared with her what I felt God was calling me to do. She said, "I know just the person you should contact. I have a friend in Georgia who is organizing a team to India; the trip will be in January or February 2010."

So, I contacted this woman named Peggy Lester. She replied to me and was willing to let me be a part of the team. We worked together to make our flights and plans on what we would carry on the trip. She was accommodating since I had no experience in this type of journey or travel.

Besides Peggy, two other women were supposed to travel with us to India. For one reason or another, these two women had to back out of the trip. Peggy and I had never met until we arrived in India. We became instant friends and became "sisters" after the three weeks we had spent together.

Peggy's original trip was to Mumbai, where she would to teach in a Christian college. One of the women who canceled earlier had asked if we could include the City of Coimbatore in our travels. She was to speak there as a representative of a ministry in which she held an office.

When she canceled, Peggy considered canceling that part of the trip. After speaking with our host in Coimbatore, she decided to keep that leg on our schedule. God was leading her because that was where I was supposed to find my connection. I asked the Lord to show me where I was to connect with my ministry partners in India.

After arriving in Mumbai late at night, we spent the night with our Mumbai host family. He would chaperon us on down to Coimbatore by train the next day.

Coimbatore would be our first stop for ministry. At the end of three days, I knew that was where God wanted me. I asked the host pastor there to pray about my call and see if he agreed. He said God had already confirmed my ministry to him. God is so amazing.

My trip with Peggy was for three weeks. Since 2010, I have traveled four times to India, extending my stay each time. I am working my way to a six-month possible stay next time, which I feel God has called me to do.

God has put such love in my heart for the people of India. Bringing them the Good News of Jesus Christ is my greatest joy. My heart yearns to go when I am not there. I am at home with my Indian family.

I am writing this testimony after my fourth trip at 70 years of age. My desire to go back to India is just as strong now as it was the first time. This last time, we could do what I call a "Walk for Jesus" through the villages. We stayed for three days and two nights. We spend quality time with the people so we can get to know them better. There is no doubt in my heart because I begin to long to return to India when I come home.

God told me ministry here in the States is just as important as my ministry in India. I am a lay person, no one special, yet God called me to do this work for Him. Just as He called His disciples who were ordinary people to Himself two thousand years ago, He is still calling lay people today. It does not matter who you are, where you come from, your age, or your gender. God will use you if you say, YES!

I have much to thank Peggy for, especially her patience with a green missionary from New York. She states she is thankful for the small part she played in my ministry as she continues to watch my growth as a missionary. I have to disagree with her words in small part; I believe she had a considerable role as God chose her as my teacher, mentor, and later sister. Of all the people in the U.S. God could have selected, He chose this woman from Georgia. I believe God handpicked her!

I am in awe that God takes His precious time to put together people to do His work. God chose this sister because He knew her, and she knows Him. As a well-traveled missionary, she knew what God wanted me to learn, and He decided she would teach me. I love to see how God works His ways, which are beyond my understanding. He knows us individually, and He continually prepares our paths before us. He helps us in all ways to succeed in what He has called us to accomplish for His glory.

Every day I love Him more as He works in my life. Peggy and I have developed a great bond since our time together, even though we are many miles apart. We continue to follow each other and communicate about our mission adventures. Thank you, Jesus, for bringing this special sister into my life who taught me how to be a missionary. (Bonnie Hurley, New York)

1. The whole purpose of discipleship is to multiply the witness of Christ. Am I investing in someone who will one day be a devoted follower of Christ? Multiplication is how the Kingdom of God grows. Am I investing myself in a disciple of Jesus who, in turn, will invest themselves one day for Christ's sake and witness?

2. If my ministry would cease, would anyone follow in my steps to continue my ministry? If not, why not? Am I willing to change this if my answer is

no? Am I willing to invest in someone, so Christ's legacy will continue after I am gone?

Ministry for the Sovereign God

As Bonnie and I traveled for three weeks all over India, from Mumbai down to the tip of India, east and west, we experienced a variety of ministries. We did prayer walking (simply praying while we walked to a new area—letting God fill us with inspiration about the people and particular needs), ministry to children in schools, many women's meetings, pastor conferences, and praying for the sick. Everywhere we went, there were occasions to be used by God in some way or another.

In the conferences, we prayed over the pastors and wives for their ministry, marriages, and families. The people of India are beautiful. I think some of the most beautiful people in the world live in India. Their country is striking as well. We rode trains most everywhere we went. It is the primary way to travel, along with the chickens and whatever other livestock they can squeeze on a train.

In India, one of the customs is not to name a baby immediately after it is born. Sometimes it is three months before they give a child a name. I was asked by my host to meet an acquaintance of his and name their baby girl. Bonnie and I were excited to experience this honorable occasion. We discussed it and decided, with the Lord's leading, to call her Abigail. We named the beautiful little girl Abigail in a sweet, small ceremony there in the home.

At one of the gatherings, I felt the Lord lead me to preach out of the book of Esther. I love this Old Testament book. I studied it intensely before going to Nigeria. Throughout this book, the message is the Sovereignty of God, even though the term does not appear at all. One of my favorites (I know, I have many favorite Scriptures) is when Mordecai, Esther's uncle, speaks these words to Esther, "Perhaps you were born for such a time as this." God chose her strategically at that time to be Queen. She held the fate of her Jewish people within her decision. Her decision was whether to be used by God or not. Therefore, she did speak up and, thus, the Jewish people were not destroyed by Haman, Mordecai's mortal enemy. God had placed her there as Queen through His Sovereign hand for this reason, to protect His people.

As I was preaching, standing to my right was my interpreter; he wiped tears and struggled to speak the Indian words. He would be composed for a few minutes and then wiping tears the next. We made it through the message and had a powerful ministry time with the congregation. After the service, I asked him if he was ok and this is what he said: "I have never studied the book of Esther even though I am a pastor. I guess I thought it was a 'women's book' to read. As you spoke, I embraced the Sovereign God in this book. He does have our lives in His hands. I see His Sovereign hand through the book of Esther now."

We serve a powerful, Sovereign God. He is in control of every circumstance in Heaven, on earth, and everywhere in between. His ways are higher than ours, and sometimes it is hard to embrace His Sovereignty; that's when we must trust He is always LOVE.

When you travel to a culture and society so different from yours, be sensitive to the Holy Spirit because the size of your God may get a lot bigger.

1. What is my definition of Sovereignty? Do I accept His Sovereignty in my life? Is He my Lord as well as my Savior?
2. Is He the same God in the U.S. as He is in India? He loves everyone just the same. Do I believe

ALL LIVES MATTER TO HIM? Do I treat them all like they matter?
3. "Lord, help me love as You love!"

A Little Girl's Destiny

*"You could become a part of someone's Calling
or destiny; prepare now."*

In 1980, our mission team arrived safely in Ciudad Victoria, Tamaulipas, Mexico. I was overwhelmed by the little village and my new surroundings, i.e., the mountains, mud, and stick-thatched huts with dirt floors, chickens running around in the yard and even in and out of the homes. These sites were foreign to me but I loved it, and I loved the people. They were warm and welcoming. At first, the little children were frightened of us gringos. There was excitement in the village due to our arrival.

This trip was my first mission, and it made an everlasting impression in my heart. Our visit had a two-fold purpose, we were 1) to construct a small wood church approximately 15' by 30' and 2) to love the children and have a semblance of Vacation Bible School with them. We brought supplies from the States to minister with the children. We purchased the supplies locally needed to build the church, and they delivered them to the building site in the village.

As we mingled during our welcoming time, a couple came forth to meet us. The mom held her limp and seemingly lifeless little girl in her arms. The dad stood close by them. It was apparent the little one was very sick. Immediately our missionary host couple gathered the team around the family to pray for their daughter. We closed in prayer, and the couple exited from our midst.

We had one week to accomplish a lot of work and ministry. I was still in awe of my surroundings, drinking it all into my heart. We set out working enthusiastically on our tasks. We had several people on our team take turns on the building project and ministering to the children. The children were thrilled with the little gifts we had brought them and excited about creating crafts. They were terrific to serve. When you have nothing comparable, the smallest gifts and articles were delightful presents for the children.

In five or six days, the little church was complete. Even though the floor was dirt, it would remain that way. As the village people began to gather at their new small church for the dedication service, the previously sick little girl arrived with her dad and mom. The little girl, walking cheerfully by her mom's side, was dressed in her very best outfit, looking adorable and healthy. We had seen the dad at the construction site during the week but had not seen the mom or the little girl. We had not received any word of the little girl's condition either.

Sometimes you will pray for people's needs and never will hear of or see the outcome. God has not called us to evaluate our prayers; we are only to pray them. He is responsible for the results that take place. Sometimes you may pray for someone's physical healing and they are not healed. We are not God, and we do not make the decisions of life and death. God does. I learned that lesson from personal experience.

The destiny of this little girl was contingent upon the obedience of our team at that moment. We prayed for her. God saw fit to answer our prayer to heal and raise her. Maybe it was for her; perhaps it was for our team. Indeed, it was for His glory, or it was for me to see my first miracle healing to increase my faith. Possibly and probably, it was for all of the above.

Our destiny depends upon obedience to the Lord as well. When He calls us to ministry, He will equip us to do what He called. We should always want it to be for His glory and never ours. If we say no, He will send someone else, but you do not want to miss that blessing of obedience.

1. How about me? Do I have hindrances to His call and obedience? List them and pray about them to the Father. Has He affirmed any directions to me today? If so, list them.

2. Have I been a vital part of someone's physical healing? How will I respond to God and the miracle of this healing?

Living Water

"You are there to share living water."

The little girl, not quite two years old, sat on top of the donkey. The water buckets were tied securely on each side of the donkey. The mom leading the donkey traveled to the closest water source to get her water needed for the day. She would have to make a return trip later in the afternoon for their evening water needs. She walked miles on foot daily, weekly, monthly; it is just a part of their lifestyle in the remote mountain area outside Victoria, Mexico.

We know water is necessary for our bodies for us to live. Our body contains a high percentage of water. Here at home, there have been times when we experienced seasons of drought, long periods without rain. In these times, we had to cut back on washing clothes, take shorter and fewer showers, and be mindful of our water usage. After seeing and experiencing this, I became more appreciative of my water source here at home.

In John 4, Jesus referred to Himself as the Living Water when He encountered the woman at the well. What does this mean to us today? If we cannot live without taking water into our bodies, does this not say we cannot live without Him? Why do we try to live without Him?

On this trip you may take, you might have an opportunity to share a cup of living water. Think about these questions below for your preparation.

1. Is my living water well full? Do I drink from Jesus daily?
2. If not, why not? Make my commitment today to drink from the Living Water. It is important to remember "I cannot share something I do not possess."

Christ the Fountain

"Come and drink from Christ, the Living Water."

Over the last few years, I have had some experiences with water. Our ministry helped provide two much-needed water sources for villages in Africa, one in Kenya and one in Nigeria. Both of these sources gave great hope to their people. I will share about the water source in Kenya here, and later you will hear about the well in Nigeria.

In parts of Maasailand outside Nairobi, Kenya, the people have to walk miles to obtain water for themselves and their livestock. It was a blessing to raise funds and connecting sources so that the village I visited would get their water source.

The Maasai are herdsmen by profession. They raise goats, sheep, and cattle. During the dry season, the water sources are hard to find. The men and young boys herding the animals are always looking for water sources. This water source provided in Naikarra has proved to be an oasis for the surrounding people, a true oasis, and not a mirage.

I made my second trip to Kenya and Maasailand in 2008. I visited this water source in the bush after its completion. The goats and cows were drinking from the life-giving water trough. The widows with their water jugs were filling them to the brim with the fresh spring water.

We, here in the States, are blessed with plenty of water sources in most locations. As I return home from trips, I observe so much waste in our country, my heart grieves. I used to tell our boys and then our grandchildren, please don't waste food; many children are starving in other countries.

The needs of other countries should touch the heart of the people in our country. We are to be involved in supplying the needs of others who cannot help themselves. The Living Water, Jesus, is offered to all, and we, who drink from His fountain, are the ones who should share. Share in meeting physical needs as well as spiritual needs.

1. Do I take for granted the blessings God has given me? Am I drinking from the living water well? Do the things I do each day quench the thirst in me?
2. Am I willing to share a cup of this *living water, spiritual and physical?*
3. "I will count my blessings today and drink deep from the living water source of Christ Jesus. Please, Lord, tell me other ways to meet the thirsty needs of others."

Seed of Truth #22
(Nigeria)

A Well for Okpo

My first trip to Okpo, Kogi State, Nigeria, Africa, was in 2006. There were so many important, exciting things that happened on this trip. The village where we would speak at a conference had approximately 350,000 people and no permanent water source or powered electricity.

One of our national contacts from Okpo informed us his people needed reading glasses. For this trip, we collected hundreds of pairs of glasses to present to their king for his people. We bought the king several other presents, one of which was a Bible. We were aware he was Muslim but felt like this is the best gift we could give him. He received the gifts with much delight. His attendants served us refreshments as he shared about the life of his people and their village.

He was quick to report to us about promises made to him for his people by previous teams from other countries in his sharing. He shared some of the promises and the nations with us. He was very cordial during our visit but was skeptical about our intentions as well. We listened attentively but were cautious not to make promises or even hints of any obligations to him. We apologized for these last teams failures and tried as best we could to make excuses for them. (Which, of course, was not our place to do, but we did anyway.)

After leaving the king, our team discussed the possibility of digging a well for the village. The first possibility was to dig a well on the pastor's ministry grounds, where we would be speaking the next few days. It seemed like the best plan to pursue. It would be a source for the village but would be under Christian supervision.

When our team returned home, one of the pastors who had been on the trip took the possibility and made it a probability. He raised funds and collected donations for the well. With the proper help and connections, we all rejoiced at the beginning of the well's digging on our national friend's ministry compound.

Its process proved to be an unbelievably long task. The digging began within months after our return home, but the well had still not provided water by our return trip in 2008.

The well was a hand-dug well. The man digging could only complete a few feet a day; the well had gotten so deep he could not breathe down in the hole for extended periods. A water hose let down to him was the source for his breathing as he dug for a limited time. Due to the depth and air conditions, it was a prolonged process.

Here in the States, we take long showers, wash clothes that are not even truly dirty, fill swimming pools, and water our lawns, etc. We are a blessed country. Do we take our blessings here in the States for granted? You bet we do. I am guilty of believing, "I am due such and

such just because I am an American…" When I serve
on the mission field, it is a reality check for me. If God
gave me what I deserved, it would be far less than what
I have or what I could ever hope to receive.

Gratitude is nearly a lost art in the U.S.A. You do
not hear "please" or "thank you" very often. "Excuse me"
or "pardon me," or other words of good manners are
sparsely used today—it breaks my heart. When we begin
to believe we are entitled or owed such and such, we
quickly forget God and His everyday blessings of breath,
life, a sunrise or a sunset, the miracle of birth, food on
our table, and the list of benefits could go on and on.

The Grace of God is receiving NOT what we de-
serve. The Bible says, it is God who gives the health to
acquire the wealth or blessings; (Deuteronomy 8:18) we
need to remember this Scripture. If the Lord gives, the
Lord can take away!

1. As I read and hear about these true stories, do
    they bring conviction to me in any way? Am I
    grateful for what God has provided for my family
    and me?
2. Maybe I should have a time of praising God and
    thanking Him for my blessings.
3. How does my view of entitlement to comfort
    stand up to a hand-dug well?

Seeing the Unimaginable

Mission work over the years has been such a joy for me. Visiting places, seeing unimaginable things at times—some funny, some not so amusing, some heart-wrenching. On our trips to Mexico, usually, we traveled in a rented motor home. We carried building materials, tools, and items to accomplish our tasks when we reached our destination.

As we reached the border, we would pray the eyes of the border guards would not see our cargo. Out of all our trips, I think only once or so did we have anything taken from us. There were several times when it costs us a few dollars to keep our loot.

Thinking back on these trips, I can only smile and say, "God did great things" before, during, and even after returning home. As we would stop along the way across the States, we shared the Gospel, left gospel tracts, and prayed with anyone the Lord brought across our path.

We would sing praises as we traveled to our destination. Once we were across the border safely, we would pray and thank the Lord for His provisions and protection. One particular time, we were traveling to the

Juan Wesley Seminary in Monterey to do some renovating and construction. After crossing the border, as we drove along, one of the girls began to ask several of us if we had seen the goats in the trees we had just passed. One of our men, a jokester at times, said: "Are you kidding me? Goats don't climb trees." She began to speak with much enthusiasm, trying to convince us all of what she had seen. This situation about the goats in the trees became the joke of the week.

We had such a fun time that week. Serving the Lord in missions can be such a delight and bring fulfillment to your life. Seeing people's lives change, becoming friends with the nationals where you go, and growing closer as brothers and sisters in Christ on the trip makes life-changing events.

On this particular "goats-in-the-trees" trip, I remember a few of the devotional times we would have in the mornings and the evenings. Different ones would share a Scripture or a testimony, and then we would pray. Some mornings we prayed for hours, and when we finished, we were all amazed at the time that had passed. God always seemed to multiply our hours so we could accomplish our daily schedule. When you put God first, He might even make the sun stand still for you as He did Joshua.

Toward the end of this trip, we took a few hours to shop and buy a few souvenirs. After our evening meal, our jokester presented a gift to our goats-in-the-trees girl. It was a braided wire tree about 8» or 10» tall with these little plastic goats sticking in the limbs. We all cracked up laughing. Then our jokester gent confessed he also had seen the goats in the low growing trees. We all had another big laugh together.

On your trip, you may be privy to seeing some unimaginable things, some funny and some serious. Scripture tells us that we may have a hard time believing if we are not in tune with the Spirit of God. Suppose you are not listening to that small voice, studying His Word, being obedient in your life. In that case, there is the possibility you could be deceived or miss an incredible blessing or miss an opportunity to be used by God. There are wolves in sheep clothing out there today lying in wait to deceive even the elect. Beware, stay close to the Shepherd's side.

I am thankful I can say I have seen the unimaginable and the unthinkable with my own eyes. Hopefully, you will see incredible or impossible events with your own eyes. God is watching and waiting for us all, and He desires to show us more than we could ever ask, think, or imagine. Seek Him earnestly and you, too, can be ready for the unimaginable or the unthinkable that awaits you in the future.

1. Am I ready to invest my faith in the unimaginable or the unthinkable? Do I have eyes to see the invisible, and do I trust God to lead me by faith?
2. Read Ephesians 3:20 and meditate on this verse.
3. Pray for eyes to see the things of God in the Spirit regarding this mission trip.

Seed of Truth #24
(Mexico)

A Blast at Camp Sierra Linda

In 1985, a team from our church joined some Alabama friends and headed out to Monterrey, Mexico, on a mission trip. We would be working on a building project at Camp Sierra Linda outside Monterrey. The men on the team would be taking care of the building projects, and the women would take care of the meals and be on clean-up detail.

First Miracle

One evening, the cooking team was working in the kitchen preparing our evening meal. When we purchased our groceries for the week, we bought a large number of carrots. We had carrots for nearly every dinner. Carrot salad, cooked carrots, raw, etc., every way you can imagine.

I cannot remember all the particulars for this evening meal, but maybe we were cooking carrots for this meal, too. Someone asked me to light the gas stove. Not having any experience with a gas stove, I continued in ignorance. I turned on the gas, went to grab the matches, lit one, and put the match down to the pilot light opening. Suddenly, there was an explosion, the gas caught fire but it didn't come forward toward me, it went back into the piping resource, sounding like a bomb going off. We not only heard it; we felt it as the mountain shook.

WOW, did I thank the Lord for His protection! Thank you, Lord; I am here to write about this incident. It could have been fatal for me as well as those standing close to me in the kitchen.

It became a funny topic after the initial shock of what could have happened to us on the mountainside. I can still experience fear when I think of it even to this day.

A Second Miracle

We had two couples from Mexico with us on this trip. Both young couples had expressed their desire to begin their families but had not been able to get pregnant. We prayed for both couples, and shortly after we returned home, God answered our prayers for them. Both couples were expecting their first child. Praise the Lord! Be careful what you pray for on your trip!

Repeatedly, trip after trip, I have been privy to seeing my God do miraculous things. I pray that as you begin your mission service, your kingdom service for our Lord, you will taste His miraculous power and miracles as well.

1. What I may consider miracles is just our Father at work doing His daily things. "If I get to see some of Your handy work, Lord, please help me not to forget to praise You?"

2. I may see some of His handy work in my planning and preparation for a trip. Help me to acknowledge even the tiny blessings of Your handy work.

3. Keep my spiritual eyes open; don't let me miss any of Your miracles on my trip.

4. I will be an encouragement to my team members by sharing with them. Sometimes the miracle might be what happens to me.

Acting Like the Devil

Once again, I was in Mexico, among village people, where my heart was so content. A young man stood far off in the distance, just watching the activities. He was there, by the trees, every time we began our day. Some of our men had tried to approach him, but every time he would run away. We discussed this young man as a team, trying to figure out his behavior.

We worked hard and long each day. This young man was always standing close to the building site but never close enough to make personal contact. He was an attractive young Hispanic man. His clothes and body were dirty. You could tell he lacked the skills of personal care and hygiene. Several days into the week and still, no one had gotten close enough to speak with him.

The nationals told us this young man was demon-possessed. At this time in my spiritual walk, I was unfamiliar with this description of the young man. This was in the early 1980s, and my walk with the Lord was only several years old.

My spiritual father and pastor, Mark Nysewander, on our team, explained what the term demon-possessed meant. He shared some of the signs: darting eyes, lack of personal contact, lack of personal hygiene, inability to communicate or connect intelligently with others, and several other symptoms. It seemed to us this young man exhibited most of these characteristics.

I was trying to digest all of this information spiritually. We all had questions about the term *demon-possessed* and this young man. Could he come to the Lord? Would he be able to be free? Was he doomed to a lifestyle like this? What would and could his destiny be? Could he be delivered from this condition?

We learned that yielding to the Holy Spirit evidences your spiritual maturity. The enemy may attack or accuse you, but he cannot possess you if you are a Christian. Sometimes we give the enemy place by not listening to God or following His will for our lives. Repentance is the key to our abiding daily with Christ. If you give the enemy any occasion through sin, he will come into your spirit and set up camp. You end up spiritually somewhere you will not want to be. Christians can be oppressed by the enemy but not possessed.

Our lives, as Christians, are evidence of the choices we have made. Joshua told God's people, before crossing the Jordan River, *"Choose you this day whom you will serve..."* (Joshua 24:14-15) God desires to be the King of our life, and He does not share the throne with the enemy or our flesh. We must make choices, allowing Him to rule and reign in our lives.

This trip was my third or fourth trip to Mexico. I had seen the Lord do some miraculous things: from getting us across the border with no problems to multiplying finances, healing children, and keeping us safe on the treacherous roads of Mexico, but this young man was a new challenge.

I would love to say God used our team to set this boy free, to bring healing to his life but it did not happen that week. We could only leave him in the Lord's hands and pray he would someday be set free to fulfill his God-given destiny. Our prayers are still affecting him, I am sure. Do not ever stop praying. God is always at work and answering prayers.

1. Have I ever met someone I thought acted like the devil or who was possessed by the devil?
2. Have I been plagued by the enemy and given him a place in my life? Does he have me in bondage in any area of my life?
3. Can I be free and live in victory? Let me answer with a substantial and outspoken "yes" to this question. "Jesus can set me free."
4. When I travel in ministry, I could come in contact with a demon-possessed person. Do I know how to minister to this person? Let this be my prayer: "I have authority in Jesus' Name to bring healing and deliverance from any sin or bondage. I will be bold and assured of my position in Christ."
5. "Lord, prepare me for the spiritual intercession You will bring across my path on any trip."

Seed of Truth #26
(Kenya)

First Adventure to Africa

My husband and I have known Jan McCray and her husband Dave for more than 30 years. We met them when Jan was a speaker at a couple's retreat Don and I attended. The Lord knit our hearts together from that very time.

Jan is an anointed, ordained preacher/teacher. She also loves mission work, specifically among the Maasai tribe outside of Nairobi, Kenya. She has been serving the Maasai through ministry for more than 30 years. From her very first trip, her heart has belonged to the Maasai.

As she became familiar with the culture, she realized the students and widows in Maasailand needed help. The young widows with many children were most in need when their elderly husbands passed away. There would be no one to provide for the family because most widows do not remarry; it is a cultural tradition.

The students cannot attend school without paying fees and wearing school uniforms. There are so many that could not get an education because of the lack of finances.

After returning home, Jan set plans in motion to help the children and the widows. She had founded a 501© (3) non-profit corporation for her ministry. When she spoke at churches and retreats, she would share about the ministry among the Maasai, and the donations given went for their support. Over the years, Jan wrote three books, and the proceeds have gone to help the Maasai students and widows.

After the retreat, I continued to communicate with Jan. My desire to go to Maasailand increased as I read about her excursions and the ministry there in Kenya. Missions had stolen my heart, not only for Mexico but for elsewhere—by this time, I had made several other trips internationally.

Jan set a date for her next mission trip to the bush. A friend of hers from Florida, myself, and Jan would be flying out in September of 2000. Our suitcases stuffed with items to give away upon our arrival. I was just beside myself with excitement for this opportunity.

We landed late in Nairobi and spent the night in town. The next morning, we would fly out in a small plane to the bush. We would land on a dirt runway maintained at a mission station. We were so crowded in the small aircraft; we could hardly see out the window. It was a 4-seater, but we were crammed in with luggage as well.

I will never forget my first sight flying over the desert. You could see the Maasai bomas (homes), hedged in by a circle of thorn bushes. It gave a whole new meaning to the Scripture, where Hosea prayed a "hedge of thorns" for protection around Gomer, his wandering wife. (Hosea 2:6)

We would be staying with an American doctor in his home located close to the medical clinic in the bush. We did have some water issues, limited lights, and no air conditioning but we were comfortable. The water resources for all the Maasai, at this time, were limited in this area. In this community area of Naikarra, I shared previously, where the well was dug, and the water trough was built.

During the day, we walked throughout the villages visiting the homes. The communities were not close in proximity. I loved it, though. I love the outdoors, and I love to walk. While early in the morning, Jan would meet with students, parents, and widows about possible support or help, my mission friend and I would walk over the desert and hills just exploring.

One morning we tracked the elephants by their droppings but never came close enough to see them. When some of the Maasai men found out about our little trek, they freaked out and told us how dangerous that had been. If the elephants had gotten downwind of us, they would have charged us, and we might not have outrun them. From then on, we stayed close and were more cautious. We still explored on our walks but not too far from the house.

This first trip to the bush made a lasting impression on me. I no longer looked at the possessions I owned, the water I drink or bathe in, or even my family the same as I had before.

The Maasai children play together with rocks, sticks, and whatever they can find to occupy their attention. They did not own a TV, have cell phones, or toys, and such. It is dark in their bomas (homes) at night, with only the fire burning in a hole in the middle of their thatched hut. They share family time, and the children are close and bond with each other. The children have more responsibilities than they should for their age but it is just the Maasai way of living. As a child, if you are large enough to carry a baby, there will usually be a baby strapped to your back or hip.

1. This trip I am about to take could radically change my way of thinking. Am I ready for that? I may learn to sacrifice a few things for the sake of the gospel or kingdom service. Am I prepared for that?

2. God requires the giving up of self to serve Him. Am I willing to pay that price? Am I ready to have my "comfort tree" shaken?

Seed of Truth #27
(Kenya)

Experiencing a Miracle

Here are a few more highlights from a trip to Maasailand in Kenya. Along with visits to widows and student's homes, Jan would speak nightly at a camp meeting held in the little block church there on the compound grounds.

Daily, people walked for miles to get to this camp meeting. They even walked from Tanzania. At night, they bedded down on the church grounds, inside the church, and in neighboring homes close to the church. Our daily schedule was full of different events. I could barely take it all in, so many memories to cherish.

In the evening, the service would begin with singing. The music still rings in my ears. Not only do I have the joys of the music but also the memories of the Maasai men and women as they jump and leap for joy during worship. Incredibly, they can jump at least 3 feet or more off the ground from a flat foot position.

Each night, Jan preached under a small light, powered by a generator. One night the generator ran out of gas during our praise and worship time, and Jan preached in the dark. The Holy Spirit still graced us with His Pres-

ence even in the dark of night. It was an electrifying service. You could sense the manifested Presence of God.

One evening, when the doctor came home from the
clinic, he informed us he had a child in the infirmary with
meningitis, and the chances of his survival were less than
10%. We went to the hospital and prayed for this child.
Within a few days, the doctor told us that he thought the
child would recover.

In the coming years, Jan and I would get to watch
this child grow. God is so good! God raised this boy from
his deathbed. It was an honor to be a part of this miracle
healing.

I remember coming home from this trip, thinking
how blessed I was to live in the U.S. These experiences
have kept me passionate about missions; I see how people worldwide have to live. It gives me opportunities
to be grateful in my life. Thankful for the blessings, but
passionate to be sure they hear the one thing they need
to know before passing from this life into eternity.

Everyone who names the name of Christ as Savior
is a minister, maybe not ordained but called to minister.
Perhaps it is giving a cup of cold water, sharing your
finances, giving of your time and talents; there are many
things to do to further His kingdom, do something!

We will all stand accountable before God the Father,
Jesus the Son through the power of His Holy Spirit, someday. What will your excuse be? I want to hear, "Well done,
good, and faithful servant, enter in the joy of your mas-
ter." How about you? Do you want to hear Him say, "Well
done"?

1. How will the lost hear without a preacher? How

will they hear unless someone goes or someone sends them? If I can make this trip, it will probably change my perspective on life here in the States. Am I ready for that?

2. How am I preparing my heart to see or experience a spiritual miracle?

3. Do I desire to hear "well done" from the Lord? Am I willing to make the sacrifices that it will take?

Seed of Truth #28
(Nigeria)

Humble Yourself

"Humble yourself, and God will lift you up."

My Nigerian missionary friend gave me and several others an invitation to speak at the Calebite conference in Okpo, Osun State, in Nigeria, Africa. This trip would be my first speaking engagement in Okpo. This trip is when we met the King of Okpo. The plans were to fly out of Lagos to Enugu, then travel for several hours by car to Okpo. Due to the travel arrangements, we decided to leave some of our luggage at our hotel in Lagos. We would carry only the clothing and items we needed for the few days at the conference.

We boarded our plane and were off on the short flight to Enugu. After takeoff, I panicked when I remembered I had left my notes in my luggage at the hotel. At this time, I was a novice at speaking to large groups. I had addressed small groups up until this time, and even then, I had used notes for my messages or teachings. (As a security blanket, you know!)

I began to pray, along with my panicking. I would love to say peace like a river came over me, all was well with my soul and that He touched me, and my fears calmed but I am honest here; I continued in a state of panic for the flight and into the evening.

Later that night, I sought the Lord, making a few short notes when I heard the Lord speak in my spirit. He said, "You are not concerned about My message; you are concerned about your delivery and how you will look to the people." Well, what could I say but, "Yes, Lord. I repent."

I realized He was correct, as usual. I humbled myself that night, and God blessed me. When you put yourself in the position of all you need is Him, He is faithful. My messages went well, I presume, as I delivered them to the masses the next day. As they say, "the proof is in the pudding," or spiritually, "the fruit is in the response by the people." I am thankful for when He wants to speak; He can even use a donkey!

One funny thing (not funny ha-ha) as we were

leaving Okpo and returning to the airport, it began rain-
ing. When the rains start in Nigeria, the roads become
slippery with oil leaks from the cars because there has
been a long dry spell. My missionary friend, a national
pastor and myself were riding in the back seat. I was in
the middle. Next to our local pastor driver, in the front
seat, were all the big gift plaques that had been made
for us as thank you gifts. I am talking 18" x 20", 1" thick,
large, heavy plaques.

We were riding along, sharing about the Lord, and
decided to sing some praise to the Lord. When our driver
hit one of the many potholes in the "expressway," I was
taking a sip from my water bottle, and water went all
over me. I made a squealing noise, and our driver turned
his head a little to see me in the back seat. I could see
straight ahead as he veered to the left of the pavement
and hit the drop-off edge. He jerked the steering wheel
to get back on the road. As he over-reacted, we began to
spin; round and round the car went, in the middle of the
expressway. During the spins, my missionary friend and
I were calling on Jesus very loudly. The vehicle landed
backward off the road, facing the opposite direction.
The large plaques were still in the front seat and had
not flown around in the car, which was a miracle itself.
Anyone of them could have caused severe injury.

Once we stopped, two young men came to our
rescue within minutes and pushed us back onto the
highway toward our destination. Where these young
men came from is a mystery; they appeared immediately and were gone just as quickly. Were they angels, I
don't know? I guess I will find out when I get to heaven,
hopefully. As we got back on our way, the local pastor

seated by me said, "Well, I guess that puts a new spin on your trip!" We all laughed after giving praise to God for our safekeeping.

I learned several vital lessons on this trip. God is always with us. First, He is our Protector, and all he wants is for us to be available; and, He will do the rest. Second is there is a Scripture that says, if we will open our mouth, He will fill it. (Psalm 81:10) We need to study and hide His Word in our heart and He will do above and beyond all we can ask, think, or imagine, according to His power, if we will allow Him to speak through us in any situation.

1. Pride in ministry will cripple my delivery to those God places before me. "Lord, help me be humble. God speak through me Your words. Make me available, and I know You will make me able. I may not have a platform to deliver a teaching message, but those I come in contact with will read me like an unspoken message."

2. "God, place Your guardrails to protect my behavior so pride will not cause a wreck in my witness for Christ."

3. "Thank you, Father, when I am doing your business, it is Your business to watch over me and keep me safe! Also, God, I trust Your promise to give me the words I need, when I need them!"

Seed of Truth #29
(Nigeria)

A Simple Pair of Glasses

As I was preparing for my second mission trip to Nigeria, I felt a strong compulsion in my spirit to purchase a pair of magnifying glasses for myself to carry on the trip. I do wear prescription glasses, and if something were to happen to them, I would not be able to read my Bible or see my notes. Therefore, as the compulsion was intense, I purchased a cheap pair of magnifying glasses. This compulsion was somewhat strange to me since I had already collected 300 pairs of glasses to give away in Okpo. However, I felt this pair would be available specifically for me if I needed them.

This trip to Nigeria would be a life-changing experience for me. It was my second trip to Nigeria but it would be the first time to attend The Calebite Conference in Okpo, Kogi State, Nigeria. This conference has an ever-increasing amount of people; the numbers have grown over the last several years to nearly 12,000 or more people. The conference gathers on top of a mountain under makeshift arbors. People come from all around Okpo and even from out of the country. They have speakers who attend from Ireland, England, Brazil, and many other places. I felt humbled and blessed to have an invitation to address the people who would be attending the conference. A well-known fact is this village of approximately 350,000 people have no running water source or electricity.

We arrived in the village, and they gave us a tour of the Ministry founded by the Pastor, a mighty man of God. He has such a heart to minister to his people in Okpo. The ministry owns several acres on which the Pastor and his family live, with schools, a church, a seminary, and a small community meeting building. After the tour of the grounds, we returned to the compound where we would be lodging. We prepared for the evening service.

As we made our way to the mountain grounds for our evening service, it was just beyond words to see the number of people walking and riding motorcycles. There was an occasional car now and then making their way to the grounds for the conference.

That night several pastors/evangelists spoke, and the response at the end of the service was phenomenal. We stayed late into the evening, and as we made our exit, someone was still preaching. Our information was they would go late into the night hours.

The next day I would be addressing the congregation. I did not know which group I would be speaking to until later in the evening. I trusted the Lord would prepare me for "whomever" I would be addressing the next day.

They assembled very early in the morning on top of the mountain—preachers, teachers, evangelists, one right after the other addressing the ever-growing number of people gathering. These people were hungry to hear the Word of God and for God to do miraculous things for them, to deliver them, to set them free, to experience salvation, and to have their needs met. God is all they have to depend on, and He always shows up for them. They truly live by faith. The Calebite Ministry even feeds one meal a day to the thousands of people who come to the conference.

The schedule is to have several preaching messages and then break the large crowd into groups, i.e., women, men, pastors, youth, and widows, etc. I was privileged to speak first to the women and then to the young adults. Wow, what an experience both were. They both were very attentive.

As I spoke to the women, my English was translated into two different languages. Translations give time to think but it is challenging to keep the anointing flowing. I trust God spoke and ministered through me because the response for prayers and ministry was fruitful.

It was a joy to address the youth because they (most of them) understood English, and I could minister to them without an interpreter. They sat so still, took notes, and it was a rewarding experience to speak to them about the Lord and Christian disciplines.

As we finished our sessions and were walking back to the vehicles that had carried us up on the mountain, a young woman around thirty years old made her way through the crowd to speak to me. Through an interpreter, she asked me, "Do you have a pair of glasses you can give to me? I can't see to read my Bible..." I was humbled, to say the least, very blessed to have listened to the voice of God and obeyed by purchasing the glasses that I had brought for myself. "Yes," I told her, "I have a pair of glasses just for you. When you return this evening to the grounds, you make your way to me, and I will have your glasses."

This whole trip had been a fairytale mission trip. Having the opportunity to speak at the conference, experience ministry in such volume, and the privilege to supply glasses for a woman who wanted to read the precious Word of God was such a blessing. Just a pair of cheap magnifying glasses can change your whole life and perspective on what God can do in your life and the lives of those you can touch in His Name IF we are obedient.

1. How important is it that I read the Bible? Am I a student of the Bible? Have I hidden God's Word in my heart so I will become more like Christ every day?
2. Obedience is vital to experience all God has for me. Listen carefully and then obey. God knows who I will meet on this trip, and He may be preparing me to meet their need.
3. "Lord, give me spiritual ears and eyes to see and hear from You."

Seed of Truth #30
(Mexico)

Listening to the Spirit

"Sometimes He speaks in a still small voice – sometimes He may sound like your own voice!"

Mission work is in my blood now. I traveled to Mexico many times to remote villages. Our mission included different building projects in various stages, i.e., laying foundations and the finishing touches to a project. Evangelism and children's ministry were usually a part of every trip.

Rev. Mark Nysewander, one of my spiritual fathers, had left our church here in the States to go to the mission field and become a teacher in a Methodist seminary in Monterrey, Mexico. We hated to lose him as a pastor, but it opened up a new area of mission work for our church. And, for that, we who loved missions were excited at the new possibilities.

With Pastor Mark now on staff at this seminary, we would make numerous mission trips to Monterrey, Mexico, with him and his family being our host and resident missionaries. Our teams over the years grew to love the students and staff of the seminary.

While we were there, we had come out on the

street to walk to another location. Most of us knew very little Spanish. We could not converse with the people on the road. We just smiled and said, "Dios de Bendigo" (God bless you) when we got the opportunity. As we passed by a storefront, a young couple sat on the steps. The mother was holding an infant around a year old. The mom was crying, and the father looked very upset, as well. The little child seemed to be asleep.

Pastor Mark stopped to converse in Spanish with the couple. He then reiterated their story to us in English. The team, hearing the translation, began pulling money from our pockets. The couple had just come from the doctor's office, where they had spent their last few pesos getting the diagnosis for their sick child. They had the prescription for the medicine but no money to get it filled.

Our hearts went out to the couple. We gave them the money and took a few minutes to pray for them. We all were thrilled to see the looks of appreciation the couple displayed. Their "gracias" (thank you) was so heartfelt and sincere.

We made our way down the street. As "gringos" walking the streets in Monterrey, Mexico, we got all kinds of reactions...some good and some not so good. We were handing out Christian tracts and greeting people as we walked.

We rounded a corner, and two young men approached us and started asking for pesos (money). Pastor Mark conversed with them, and they became hostile, and speaking aggressively. I think, at that point, our team was glad we could not understand Spanish. As they talked to us, we could not help but smell the scent of alcohol on their breath. In a few minutes, they were on their way, hollering at us as they walked down the street, calling us gringos and whatever else, I am not sure!

Pastor Mark turned to us and gave us a vital spiritual lesson. In ministry, you must learn to discern when to give and when not to give. Sometimes giving can thwart God's destiny He has planned for a person. He might be trying to teach them a spiritual lesson, bring them to Himself, change their direction, or bring them to Himself through discipline.

The use of spiritual gifts is very needed to have the mind of God. The gift of discernment is necessary for ministry. It can also be a vital part of fulfilling someone else's destiny. Ask God for wisdom and ministry gifts. God says we have not because we ask not, but be sure to ask for the right reasons.

1. Discernment is a ministry of the Holy Spirit. Am I familiar with this spiritual gift, and how vital this ministry gift is? I must be sensitive to the Holy Spirit and listen to Him as He shares His wisdom with me. Pray unceasingly.

2. Listen intently and obey immediately. Can I share an incident in which I knew the Holy Spirit used me in a discerning way?

Seed of Truth #31
(Costa Rica)

In Her Own Little World

"Communication without words is possible!"

She had a twinkle in her eye, and she stood as close to me as possible. Even though she could not speak, we communicated. She loved to hold my hand, and in my mind's eye, I can still see her looking up at me. I have a precious picture I treasure that captures her look.

Tina (not her real name) was around 12 years old and lived in the mountains of Los Guidos in Costa Rica. She had a normal birth and seemed to be doing very well before going home with her mom. For some precautionary situation, the doctors felt it necessary to keep her on oxygen. I did not learn all the details due to translation issues but I did find out there was an accident. Somehow, the oxygen machine malfunctioned and Tina's body received a traumatic shock.

In February of 1988, I had come with an evangelism mission team to San Jose, Costa Rica. We were visiting from door to door and ministering to all who would listen as we shared about Jesus. During our visits, I met Tina. She welcomed us into her little tin/wood home for our visit with her family. Her mom shared her story with us.

As Tina grew, her mom realized she had physical issues. She was slow in learning everyday things; she did not accomplish them—talking was one. She knew who she was, knew her family, and seemed to be very smart in her surroundings.

I so desperately wanted this young girl to receive a healing. I prayed and prayed that God would touch her and heal her body. The team prayed for her also. She seemed to be captive in this little body with no way to express herself except with the twinkling in her eyes.

Our team returned several times to visit in her home area. Each time we arrived, she would come and walk beside me as we made our visits all over their community.

She seemed to be comfortable in her lifestyle. Tina did not go to school because this was an underprivileged area of Costa Rica. The schools were small, crowded, and not equipped for the term of special needs children.

The houses in this area were small and made out of tin. The places had limited electric power and water resources. Tina just hung around the home in her little world.

Would this be Tina's destiny, a beautiful girl, smiling, pleasant, trusting, and happy go lucky, living her life on the side of the mountain in Los Guidos? I wish I knew the answer to that question. I did not then and still do not.

I have not been back to Costa Rica, but I often think of Tina and wonder how her life is now. She would be over 40 years old. Surely for someone who does not have all of their mental capabilities, God will bring them home as His child. Surely, He will; that is my prayer for Tina.

Maybe you know someone like Tina. God knows them, too. We can ask why, but we still trust our loving, Heavenly Father when we do not get an answer. He is Sovereign and someday, we will know the answers. He gives us the responsibility to pray and share Jesus, either by word and or deed. He calls us to reflect the love of Jesus. He can and will take care of those special people who are handicapped physically and mentally.

An Added Blessing

Another great blessing on this trip (besides meeting Tina) was the privilege of meeting Steve Green. Yep, that is right, the one and only contemporary Christian music artist. He did a concert there in San Jose. I am not sure who had the influence enough to meet him personally and spend time with him but we did get that opportunity. He is an awesome man, humble, and just glows with the love of Jesus. We were there to offer counsel at the end of his concert. What a joy and privilege that was!

1. From the small young girl to a well-known singer, I may never know who God might bring across my path on a mission trip. I must be ready to minister the love of Jesus to whomever God brings across my path. Am I ready?
2. Sometimes I will not see an answer to my prayers; I must pray them anyway. I must be faithful to do my part, and God will do His.
3. God knows my heart. He will affect my life forever if I keep my heart open.

He Finished Well

"A true hero of the faith remembered."

We arrived home in the early part of the week from Cuba. Papa John and his youngest son left home for a father/son camping trip. They decided, as part of their camping adventure, to take a rafting trip one day.

They arrived at the Nantahala River, received their instructions, made their preparations, and pushed off the bank. They were on their way for their adventure. Shortly after leaving the bank, their raft lodged on a rock. Papa John told his son to stay in the raft. He jumped out to dislodge the raft. Tragically, that was the last time Jonathan saw his Dad. The dislodged raft floated down the river with its single young passenger. At the end of the trip, Jonathan got out of the raft, called his Mom, and said, "I do not know where Dad is." She told him to tell the people, and the hunt for Papa John ensued, taking nearly all day long.

Finally, after stopping the water flow upstream, the staff found his body draped over the rock, where he first got out of their raft; his leg caught in between the large stones causing him not to free himself.

His family and our church family were all in shock at the loss of Papa John. "The Rock" was Pastor John's nickname in their family. He indeed was a hero of the faith. His family has missed him, and all that knew him experienced his loss. We loved him very much; to us all, he was the epitome of a devoted follower of Jesus.

Pastor John was only in his early sixties. He and his wife, Judy, had taken a cruise earlier in the summer to celebrate their fall anniversary of 40 years of marriage. God has numbered our days. This cruise was a great blessing for John and Judy.

"Why," everyone kept asking, "Why?" However, we received no answers. We received comfort for our pain in this loss of a dear husband, father, pastor, friend, and brother in Christ.

Long life on this earth is not promised us but God assures us He will be with us and take us to live with Him at the end of our life. Every minute of every day, we should live as if it were our last.

There was a contemporary song popular at this time called "Blessed Be the Name" by Matt Redman; a line says, "You give, and take away, blessed be Your Name."

This song gave comfort to us all, knowing that we serve the Sovereign God of the universe, and, even though we did not understand the loss, we could still trust the Love of God. We receive good things, and we are thankful and, sometimes, we experience pain, and we should be grateful as well. No, we do not understand, but we trust in our God, who loves us eternally.

1. Do I have a "Rock" in my life? Who are the examples that cause me to love and serve Jesus more? What characteristics will it take to live life on a mission for Christ?

2. Who are my fallen heroes? What are some impressions they made on me?

3. What impressions am I making on others?

Leaving a Legacy

In 2007, our church sponsored a family mission trip to Jamaica. I was excited to accompany Kayla, our grand-daughter, and Jordan, our oldest grandson, on this trip. They were in middle school at this time.

Our mission ministry was mainly to visit orphanages and hospitals on the island. Kayla and Jordan would go into these orphanages, pick those kids up and play with them, and tote them around on their hips. It was such a joy to see their behavior.

As we pulled into the driveway of one of the orphanages we were to visit, I will never forget that we were overwhelmed with what we saw. There were so many children and adults in our view, lying on mats, sitting in wheelchairs, being held by their caregivers; the sight stirred up all kinds of emotions in our hearts.

The bus stopped, and we prepared to exit. Jordan stood and looked down at me in my seat and said, "Gran, I don't know if I can do this or not." I spoke to him from my heart, "Jordan, I feel the same way you do." Within several minutes after exiting the bus, Kayla and Jordan were consumed with kids, pushing their wheelchairs, playing ball, holding their hands, listening to the children, and carrying on conversations. It all was a beautiful sight to me.

We visited the bedridden children. We prayed and played with all of the children as best we could, overlooking their handicaps. The caregivers were so attentive to the children. The calling to be a caregiver has to be straight from God. I am sure they will receive a reward for their love, diligence, and care.

This orphanage was for the throw-away children. The founder heard the Lord's call to find the children on the island nobody wanted. Her home would be for children deformed, mentally handicapped, abandoned, misused, and unloved children. She found many of these children left on the garbage heaps in and around Montego Bay, Jamaica.

On the front grounds, the children live, and there are gates for safety from the back property, where adults needing special care live. Most of these adults had lived in the home since childhood; it was all they knew as home.

Kayla and Jordan interacted with these children doing what they could do best. One mentally challenged teenage girl loved to sing, and she kept singing the song, "This Little Light of Mine," repeatedly. Kayla connected with this girl, and they spent a large portion of the time together.

Out of all the trips I have ever made, sharing this trip with Kayla and Jordan will be a memory I cherish. Seeing how they responded to these children in this home and the others, I hope, helped shape their life views and broaden their love and acceptance for all kinds of people.

I pray this trip was instrumental in Kayla's desire to become a nurse. I might add that she passed the State Board Nursing Examine just a few days ago and is now a Registered Nurse. We are so proud of her. She is now married with a son of her own, who is three years old. Little Colton is such a joy for Don and me. Jordan still loves children today. This coming March, in 2021, he will be getting married to Carlee in Jamaica. Jordan loved the island, so they will be sharing their vows at Sandals Resort. Who knows, I may make a trip someday with one of them in charge? Wouldn't that be a great experience?!

1. It is good to introduce youth to mission service early. God can speak to them to become full-time or part-time missionaries for Him.

2. Would I be willing to invest in youth, sponsor a youth, or accompany teens on a trip?
3. To what ages do I feel I can best minister and relate?

The Grace River of God

One of my favorite Scriptures is Ezekiel 47; it deals with water and rivers. This Scripture is a metaphor for God's River of Grace. Let me share personally with you for a minute.

I have been thinking about this Grace River in my life. Ezekiel 47:3 states the water is first ankle-deep. To me, this is the picture of my salvation. I took my first step, not knowing much but desiring to enter a relationship with Jesus. I think I stayed in the ankle-deep water for a long time. God was faithful and met me there continually but He eventually began to call me out deeper.

As I grew spiritually, the deeper water began beckoning me to venture into water over my knees, then to my waist, and then I was over my head and could not touch the bottom. Nor did I want to reach the bottom. God's grace has no cellar or roof, and there is always more in this Grace River.

Using this metaphor of being in deep water reminds me of an experience with my brother on vacation. I was maybe fifteen, and he around ten. We were floating on two rafts close to each other. All of a sudden, I realized I could not touch the bottom. My brother did not know enough to recognize what was happening. I am thankful God gave me the wisdom to push my body down, hit bottom, and come up under the floats, moving them toward the shore. My parents had no idea we were in peril. I finally told them many years later. I shared with my brother as well as how scared I was and our situation's potential danger. I remember the fear that gripped me. To this day, the ocean is a wonder but still a fearful creation to me.

I shared with Pastor Brian about feeling like I was out of a boat, in deep waters; I had an invitation to speak at a large conference in Nigeria. I will never forget what he said to me, "Jesus will meet you there in the deep." Pastor Brian was correct because God has always been faithful to meet me wherever and whenever I am doing His will.

Once you have experienced the "deep river of God's grace," you can never be happy in the ankle-deep water again. Yes, it can be scary when you cannot touch the bottom, and you are not in control; but there is nothing more satisfying than to be in the mighty, rushing current of God's great River of Grace. This position is where you learn total dependence. I do not ever want to go back to ankle-deep.

Jump in; the River of Grace is great! It is the only way you will be able to experience His grace. God is patient; He is continually calling you to the depths of spiritual growth. Missions are the raft that will put you out in the deep. Go for it, be all in; He will meet you there, wherever there is!

1. When I enter the River of Grace, I might not be

able to touch the bottom, but be sure of one thing, when I am on a mission for Him, He is close by me. Do I have control issues? How will I respond when I am not going to be in control in an international setting?

2. Where do I think I will have the weakest time trusting God's Presence to be with me? Will it be when I cannot control things and trust myself to the Sovereign God who holds me in His hands?

Seed of Truth #35

Living Your Dream

As I returned from the dentist one day, I got behind a vehicle pulling a horse trailer. These words were on the back of the trailer: "Livin' the Dream." My mind began to twirl; what does that mean? The following is the inward conversation I had with the Lord.

"Livin' the Dream"...just what does that mean? It may mean a lifestyle that you will someday wake up from and then come face to face with a rude REALITY. All you thought was fun, happiness, and fulfillment could be a nightmare and not a dream. Why? Because dreams do not last; we eventually wake up from them. People here in the States and even around the world use the term "The American Dream." They say, "I want it, and I should have it, and I will do whatever it takes to get it."

What is worth living or dying for today? The older I get, and the more I see change, it makes me nostalgic. I find myself looking for something that was a dream or a reality in the past. We all want the best of everything and hope we do not have to experience any pain to get all we want. Nevertheless, we know this is not the usual pattern of how things happen.

If you think you are living your dream life, be careful, you might wake up to find it to be the nightmare that ruined your life. Jesus came to give us life and life more abundantly. It is only in Him; we will find true happiness, fulfillment, and joy. There is a peace and constant joy that cannot be taken from you. The world didn't give it to you, and the world cannot take it away unless you give it up.

I have found such fulfillment in mission service for the Lord. I hope and pray that He continues to call me into His fields that are white unto harvest. I do know people that have made one mission trip, and it changed their life focus. I also know a few who say they will never go again go on a trip and are critical of people who do. Which will you be?

God works in the hearts of people in different ways. However, know this one thing for sure; God's heart is mission service ministry, local or foreign. Learn what God wants you to learn and leave other people's life in His hands. Live your dream because you are accountable for what you do with your life.

1. What is my dream? Do I believe my vision can become a reality?
2. Why do I think God has called me to be part of a team and a mission trip?
3. Am I willing to let Him give me His vision to come to pass, or do I want to stay in control of my life?

Seed of Truth #36

"Here I am, Lord,
BUT send someone else!"

If you do not know my favorite Scripture is Isaiah 6:8, my life verse, here it is: "Here I am, Lord, send me." I love the story of how God spoke; Isaiah listened and answered God by volunteering to go for Him. God touched his lips with hot coal, purified his heart and lips. God gave him the privilege of ministering to His people. I have made this my answer to God for many years, "Send me, send me, Lord."

I am sure your faith has been tested if you have served the Lord for any time. One week I received a call, and this friend told me she had a friend whose mom was terminally ill. This daughter asked her if she knew anyone who could come and pray with her mom because she was at death's door.

My friend thought of me and called me. I was humbled. I am sorry to say though my first reaction was, here I am, Lord, AND I will help YOU find someone to go to see this dying woman. I felt convicted immediately by the Spirit. I heard Him say to me, "You are always praying, 'Here I am, Lord, send me,' what about this time? What about this woman and her need for prayer?" The Spirit moved me, and immediately I repented and committed my service to the Lord for this woman.

I had the privilege to pray with this sweet woman and her husband. I appreciated so much the Presence of the Lord with us in their home. Several weeks had passed when I heard she had received her final reward. If you have not been in the presence of someone very close to passing, it is a humbling experience? The Manifested Presence of the Lord is mighty, bringing His comfort and peace.

Many times in our lives, we hear the Lord whisper, "Will you go for Me?" Don't let those gentle nudges from the Spirit pass by. There is nothing like obeying His voice to go for Him.

1. How about my commitment to the Lord; am I willing to go for Him, speak for Him, live for Him, and if need be, die for Him? Each day in many places around the world, Christians give their lives for Christ. How about me?
2. Will I live for the One who died for me? Will I answer, "Yes, Lord, here I am, send me?" Meditate on Isaiah 6.

From Beauty to Bondage

Lessons Learned on the Road!

My hubby and I were headed home from a vacation down in Florida. It had been a relaxing time of just doing nothing. On our way home, I could not help but notice the Spanish moss hanging in the trees as we drove toward the Georgia state line.

I began to enjoy its beauty and how pretty it looked. As we continued down the road, I began to notice where the moss was so heavy in the trees; the trees looked like they were dead or dying.

I did a little research on Spanish moss via Google, and this is what I learned. Spanish moss has no roots but is an air-born plant. The moss spreads through blowing in the air, and wherever it attaches, it can grow. Birds also use it for their nests, so it travels from tree to tree via the birds. When a tree gets so full of moss, it takes over the life of a tree. The tree dies. What begins as a little and looks nice becomes a lot, eventually strangling the health from a tree.

So, what is so interesting about this? I began thinking about our lives regarding sin. Even though we have the root of evil through inheritance, sin is in-born, thanks to Adam and Eve. Everywhere we turn, we see the decline in Godliness and holiness from commercials on the TV about clothes, food, and cars, etc. A beautiful woman's body today is even an enticement for you to purchase a hamburger. The enemy is very subtle. He will use every open door to entice you into sin.

Where am I going with this? The gift of life and beauty can travel from attraction to bondage. What God meant for beauty, holiness, and our best, the enemy distorted and is using to entice the world for evil. Through our weaknesses and fleshly desires, we keep falling into the same traps of sin. Beauty can become bondage if not treasured by us as a gift from God. The purity of life and morality are gifts from God. Please do not throw them away; do not live in the flesh either; bondage will be the outcome, and death will soon follow.

Many people in the areas I have traveled have fallen into bondage to the enemy and flesh. How will these people hear about Christ's freedom unless someone goes and tells them the good news? Is God calling you for such a task? It may be just a short-term trip, or it might be a lifelong calling.

1. If God asks me to go, what will my answer be? What will cause me to say "no"?
2. Do I need freedom from any bondage in my life that will allow me to decide to go? Do I have some Spanish moss in my life?

Seed of Truth #38
(Bolivia)

Doors of Opportunities

As we flew over the mountains before seeing the city of Tarija, Bolivia, my friend Karen McLaughlin and I discussed who would take the gospel to all the little villages positioned on the sides of the mountains. We could see small settlements here and there; our hearts stirred with this thought. We asked the question, "Who will go to them and tell them about Jesus?" Jesus knows they are there but who else does? Who else cares?

This beautiful city nestled between the mountains where the clouds roll over the plateaus is a lovely sight. Tarija translated is, "The City of Smiles," and rightly so. These people are so warm and friendly, open to every newcomer.

I believe Tarija, Bolivia, is one of my favorite places to minister. The people are hungry to come to the Lord and grow in Him, as well. One of the things happening in their culture is very disturbing to me. It is almost like a warning signal of something that could take place in our country someday. It is a city that has a very active demonic and occult activity among its people. They need Jesus in their city and especially in their homes.

Each time I have been to Tarija, I spent many days and hours counseling married women, young women, and men. The most needed counseling is in the areas of marriage and relationships. It is heartbreaking what is taking place in their culture. Men and women leave their families and are unfaithful. Men father children out of wedlock. Many are also in bondage to pornography and drugs. Promiscuity is rampant among adults and teenagers.

The laws in Bolivia are very strenuous where marriages are concerned. You must pay and file for separation papers, and there is a very long waiting period before you can obtain a divorce. Many families and marriages are in crisis. They need the holiness of God and the love of the Lord Jesus in their lives and homes.

We have an opportunity for ministry in Bolivian schools and colleges. The government has opened the doors for many opportunities to bring healing to their hurting people. Drugs, alcohol, witchcraft, and even gangs are significant issues in this beautiful little mountain country. The yielding to sin causes open destruction and snowballs into every area of their lives. They need Jesus. Who will go and tell them about Jesus?

I am so thankful for the Whitley's introducing me to ministry in Peru and Bolivia. We must go to places that have slim opportunities to hear about Jesus. Will you go?

1. The Bible says, how can they hear without a preacher? Who will send the preacher? (Romans 10:14–15) Maybe God is calling me. What will my answer be? Will it be, "Yes, I will go"?
2. Can I see any correlation between the culture in Bolivia and the U.S.?
3. Who will share the hope of the gospel here in the U.S., will I?

Seed of Truth #39
(Jamaica)

A Special Friend

"Hearts knit together in service for the King."

Do you remember my sharing about the women's retreat that impacted my relationship with Jesus? I would like to emphasize another occasion I experienced, which is similar.

There are opportunities for women who have attended such a weekend to serve and minister on other scheduled weekends. Such an occasion arose down in Jamaica. A friend gave me the leader's name, Patti Jo Bach. She would be the lead layperson organizing the team. I love Jamaica, and I love doing ministry there whenever I get the opportunity.

I contacted Patti Jo (better known as PJ), and we immediately hit it off as sisters in the Lord. Over the next few months, her team spent time together in preparation for the Jamaica weekend. That weekend was the first occasion of many special times I would get to serve with PJ.

PJ, by trade, is a Registered Nurse (RN). Over the last few years, she began serving on the mission field in many different areas. Our hearts bonded as we shared our experiences of being on mission for Jesus, especially in Africa. She loves Africa as I do.

Since our meeting, we shared in Jamaica women's ministry many weekends. Since 2010, after my ordination, I served as a Spiritual Director for the retreats—as a member of the clergy for the women along with several other ordained ministers, male or female.

One of our trips to Jamaica happened when a hurricane was crossing the island; there was torrential rain, which produced cooler temperatures. PJ and I had carried light clothing and light bedding, expecting warm weather. I will never forget how we dressed for sleeping at night in our unheated rooms. We wore as many layers of clothing as we could get on our bodies. We laughed and took silly pictures of each other; serving Jesus can be so much fun at times.

In 2011, PJ and I, along with a team, had the privilege of traveling to Denmark to serve on a women's team. Whenever and wherever we have traveled together, it has brought us closer as sisters in the Lord.

PJ now serves as a prayer warrior for the ministry God has given me. She lives about an hour from me but we keep in touch often and get together when possible. PJ, as an RN, offers her talents to camps for children and teenagers. She is making small strides into these lives for Christ.

Missions, whether in Judea or the uttermost parts of the world, are God's heartbeats. Jesus came that we might have life, and that is our story; wherever PJ and I get an opportunity to share, we want to be faithful to God's call on our lives. God may change your direction for a different season; He wants you to be available at all times to give an account of the hope that lies within you. He will equip you with His Holy Spirit for the task; we always need to be ready.

1. Do I have a PJ in my life, a special someone who shares my love for Christ and is willing to share and support me, wherever and whenever God calls? I need those real friends, sisters, and brothers in the Lord. I thank God for those who love and support me right now.

2. A new lifelong Christian friend might be on the mission field waiting to make my acquaintance; they may be down the road or a few miles from my home. We, as friends in Christ, are supposed to do life together. "Lord, help me find those special friends You have for me. I will invest in their lives as You, Christ, invest in ours."

Know Thyself

The more you know about yourself, the more you will understand how to minister on mission for Jesus.

In 2012, a Romanian couple invited me to go on a mission trip to Romania. The ministry on the trip would be very different from any trip I had been on before. Being open and listening to the Lord, I agreed to make the trip with them. I love new adventures, and I would get to do something I had a passion for on this trip.

The main object of the ministry would be to give eye exams to people in need. We then fitted them with a pair of suitable donated glasses we had brought with us. We were hoping we would have a variety of vision strengths needed to meet everyone's needs. We would be holding these clinics in churches that had previously signed up for this ministry. We had three people on the team certified to give eye exams.

After they had received their glasses, their last meeting was with me; I was their checkout point person. I would introduce myself and chat with them lightly for a few minutes. I would ask if they had received glasses and if they were pleased with them. We talked about their family, and so on.

I would then move into a more in-depth discussion with them, letting them know we not only care about their physical needs but we care about their spiritual needs, too. This discussion opened the door for me to share about Jesus with them. Not all were open but a lot of them were.

I shared how much God loved them and that He wanted a personal, intimate relationship with them. They shared with me many needs and the hardships of their lifestyle there in Romania. My heart went out to them because of their situations.

I did share with them that God knew where they were, and He knew their needs. However, when the doors of their hearts would open, I would tell them of the home God was preparing for them in heaven. Also, I shared we are only passing through this life for a short time, and our eternal home is the most crucial thing in our future. Most listened very intently as I told about Jesus, salvation, and the repentance God requires from all humankind to be in a relationship with Him.

I was blessed to pray with 76 people during this time. Fourteen of them prayed to receive Jesus as their Lord. What a joyful time we had rejoicing each evening as we prayed for our new brothers and sisters in the Lord.

We also held several Vacation Bible Schools with the children and joined in various revival services where we had opportunities to share our testimonies and pray with people. God moved in remarkable ways, and I am delighted to have been a part of this team and ministry.

I learned about myself that week, or maybe, I should say I relearned this: I am bolder in my witness for

Christ when I do not know the person with whom I am sharing. I am not sure I like this attribute in myself either, nor whether it pleases the Lord. I am still praying about this!

Yes, we must be bold on the mission field. I agree with that for sure. What bothers me the most about this is how hard it is to share with the people I love, like good friends and especially family. Knowing there is a hell where people will go for eternity if they do not receive Jesus ought to drive me and you to share Jesus with them. It should inspire us to talk with anyone living and breathing, should it not? I, as the author, am not the only one confessing here, am I?

1. How about me? Am I bold in sharing Christ and His love with those I meet?
2. Why do I fear rejection? Should not my love for these people and where they will spend their eternity be the issue here?
3. What will my commitment be for this trip? Will I share boldly? What about when I come home, will I do the same?
4. "Lord, fill me with the power of Your Holy Spirit that I might be bold here at home and wherever You take me."

Seed of Truth #41

Investing in the Younger Generation

Shortly after our two sons married, Don and I began investing in young couples' lives and marriages. Our two sons, their wives, and several of their friends in young marriages attended our get-togethers. I would do the primary research and compose the teaching, and I would teach. If it was a sensitive study, Don and I would both handle the lesson. I would cook dinner for the couples, and after fellowshipping over the meal, we would have the teaching. I would have to say out of all the ministry I have done, this is one I find very fulfilling. After nearly 55 years of marriage, I think Don and I have some vital information for couples that will enrich their relationships.

If I wasn't traveling in mission work, we usually were meeting weekly and monthly with couples. We learned a lot in these months and years and treasured these friendships. Most young adults attending our groups now have children, grown children, and even a few have grand-children. We still see some of them, and it has been a joy to love and fellowship with them, watch their families grow in their walk with the Lord.

Investing in young lives has always been important to me, especially if they are family or close enough to feel like family. Don and I have always been young at heart. We played our last softball games when we were in our 60s. I told Don, "I am going out like Moses, with my eyes not even dimmed." I didn't want to be one of those old people as I got older just to "meet and eat" because I still have many items on my bucket list to accomplish. I want to hear, "Welcome home, good and faithful servant." I want to accomplish all God has destined and called me to do.

1. If I do not feel that God has called me to an international ministry, maybe working with young people could be my calling.
2. Do I have a good rapport with younger people or children? I will pray about this.
3. How important is it to me to raise Godly children for the Lord?

It's Time for a Home

Several years ago, after making a few trips to Kenya, I began to desire to see my Kenyan friends again. I couldn't stop wondering what they were doing and how their lives were thriving, etc. I contacted Jan McCray to ask her to help me plan a trip. Jan was no longer able to travel that distance due to her health. She was quick to tell me that God had been speaking to her about it being time to build an orphanage there in Maasailand. She was so excited that I wanted to go, and we began the preparations for me to make a trip.

As she had begun praying about this adventure, God had given her the name of a couple she would ask to be the directors of the home. I knew the couple from the first trip I had made with Jan. After the couple agreed to run the household, plans began to fall in place. We knew God was in it when this young couple said they had been praying for the children in the bush who were orphaned. Because Jan had been an integral part of the Maasai people's lives and helped so many there in the bush, the chief gave the property where we would build. Jan's board, of which I am a part, approved the project, and we were ready to roll.

Jan drew a pencil diagram of her vision building. She sent it to me, and I passed it along to my son, who does drafting for a living. After his rough drawings, we sent it to my cousin, who added a few updates and details. The plans were finished and presented to and approved by the Jan McCray Ministries Board.

The young pastor and his wife, who would be running the home, started to work arranging contractors. This building would be a monumental task. The road to the villages is not paved or kept, with trenches, rocks, and is horrible. To get big delivery trucks with lumber and other building materials would be a challenge. Also, to make matters harder, there is no electrical power in the bush.

The House of Love was finally completed in 2013, after many months and a few setbacks. It has approximately 5,000 square feet and able to house 30 or more children. I traveled there to finalize some of the arrangements before the opening of the home. It is a beautiful big home sitting on the side of a hill next to the roadside. A small grammar school, a medical clinic, and a church are just down the road, a perfect location for a children's home.

Over the last several years, I have traveled several times to Kenya as the board representative. As of the writing of this devotion, we have 33 girls living in the home, our caregivers, and their children. We would take orphan boys but they do not give up their boys in the bush; it is a male-oriented culture. Twenty years have passed since my first trip to Kenya, and I have come to love the Maasai people so much. These trips have been one of my most treasured highlights of ministry.

1. I need to think seriously about a trip that has no modern conveniences for me. How will I make out in this environment? There are no internet connections, no hot running water, and a long treacherous ride over a mountain to reach a road unmaintained and uncomfortable to travel, and no night lights but the stars. Is a trip like this for me?

2. What price am I willing to pay to minister for Jesus' sake? I must count the costs.

Seed of Truth #43
(Southeast Asia)

Preparation is Mandatory

Testimony by Melissa Beasley

I am not a full-time missionary. I understand, though, that God has given me a heart for service to others and a special love for children and their development. My church extended an invitation to join a small team traveling to Europe to serve missionaries and their children while attending a conference. I did not need to think twice before saying, "Yes!"

We would be facilitating pre-planned activities for an assigned group of children for the week; and sharing Christ through worship, communication, and play. It sounded perfect for me, and I privately hoped I would be a good match for my assigned group. The children currently lived with their "global servant" parents who minister in the surrounding areas. Three of us, as team members, were asked to lead worship for the children each day—a simple task, but certainly one that needed some level of preparation. Each lady had unique talents that contributed to the children's worship experience, and two had experienced previous mission work opportunities. I had no international mission experience, so I was excited to learn what I needed to help make the week a memorable experience for these children.

Because of security issues, many of the children worship in homes, not churches. Most do not attend the public school system, although some do. For sure, they do not have the opportunity for a typical Sunday school kids experience. The heat was on to give these kids a great experience and to give away the ending—we did! It was not without sacrificing sleep, individual preferences, and a bit of ego and pride for our worldly-filled, but Christ led, adult-team.

I learned that preparing for a "mission" experience begins at the time of invitation. I committed and took it seriously.

I questioned what this commitment looked like, *to* me, and *for* me. Also, what should it look like for the team? Do I need to be different somehow to be worthy of this single call to serve? Am I qualified personally or spiritually for this task?

Once I asked the questions, I turned from inward to upward—in trust and faith. Heartfelt humility went upward in prayers for quickness in understanding, the ability to be gracious, mainly with our adult team's diversity, even with little sleep—prayers for safe travels and a Christ-centered, fun, and memorable experience for the children.

We ladies immediately faced some challenges in providing the children's worship, low sound volume, lyrics that some of the kids hadn't known, and even a bit of "judgment" about lack of preparation that crept its way into our days. Yes, we are human, doing God's work, in an unfamiliar country!

Confined nightly in a single hotel room with a king

bed for two and an available cot for one, God did not judge us for falling short, but instead, He softened our hearts with His gift of laughter. We prayed, and we laughed as we allowed God to smooth the jagged edges of each day. In the end, it was ultimately our commitment to do this service for God that saw us through the week. There is no doubt that this was true for each of our team members.

In its initial appearance, the commitment seemed a simple task of providing a fun service to kids; but mind you, it was challenging to face and correct the heart challenges that can and did inevitably occur while on this mission for God. I realize now that understanding what I read in the trip booklet and what I experienced can be different. It answered my question, "What does this commitment look like on me?" Well, I get to choose my response to every challenge; I'm free to every path of response available. In that short week, I recalled that my commitment to God as the goal ALWAYS makes it easier to choose the right answer. I am grateful that when I allow God, He makes it so easy!

The children in my group, ages 5 and 6, were smart, funny, and beautiful! They sang and ran and followed the song motions during worship, played and collected rocks in the sea surf, and swung on the playground swings. They colored and decorated masterpieces of art from construction paper. They were kind and curious; healthy kids seem to crave that same inclusivity and acceptance that we adults also need. They hugged us a lot!

The children left their conference soulfully enriched with music, art, play, and lots of love! Their par-

ents enjoyed learning and singing and being together
with their missionary friends.

We, the adult team, grew spiritually, somewhat pain-
fully, alongside sacrifice and laughter.

It seems as God uses us to do His work on a mission, things rarely happen as we would expect. His way
is always of excellence as He is excellent; therefore, He
stretches us beyond our own perceived and comfortable limitations. The Holy Spirit within us serves others
while simultaneously refining our dark places into silver
and purifying them like gold. In doing so, He answers
my question, "Do I need to be different somehow to be
worthy of this single call to serve?"

Despite us, His mission NEVER fails when we com-
mit to doing the will of God, which is to reveal Jesus to
the world.

Peggy: This devotional is by my special friend,
Melissa Beasley. We experienced her first international
mission trip together. I can say an emphatic "Amen" to
her devotion. Sometimes your trip will not turn out the
way you expect, but if you lift the results and expectations to the Lord and move in His Spirit of co-operation,
He will always take care of the outcome for those ministered to through the ministry.

1. Am I taking prayerfully and seriously this responsibility since I agreed to attend this trip?
2. Is there something in my heart that might prohib-
   it a smooth and profitable result from this trip?
3. Am I willing to forego my expectations and allow the Lord to filter down blessings to bless
   them through my obedience? This trip is not

about me!
4. Who should get the glory from my ministry? Me
   or God?

Visit Me in Prison!

Missions for Jesus have many different facets. Several years ago, I had an acquaintance ask me if I would be interested in serving in prison ministry. Little did this person know I had a desire for years to get involved in prison ministry. Years earlier, I had served in detention ministry for youth. Now, an invitation was before me to minister to the incarcerated women in maximum security prisons. I jumped at the offer with both feet.

During the time serving in the youth detention, I will share that I would like to slap some parents. Sorry, just being honest here. Some of these hurting youth needed a heart healing. They needed counseling and their hearts healed from things they had experienced or not experienced as a youth. When the going got rough, these parents just bailed and called authorities to pick them up because they couldn't deal with their behavior. I wonder how many times God has wanted to bail on us for misconduct and behind the scenes behavior! But He is faithful. Sorry to say, sometimes it is the parents that need help and healing. They have passed their hurt and unhappiness on to their children because they did not seek help.

In 2017, I began serving as a member of the clergy on teams to minister on a Kairos weekend. We had team meetings for several months before holding our weekend. I had never been involved in any ministry as heart-wrenching but fulfilling. Thinking back to my youth detention ministry, I am now involved with adult women who have unresolved hurts, probably from their youth, that progressed into breaking laws. Would you like to be involved in this much-needed ministry? It is an excellent opportunity to serve.

Jesus' words in Matthew 25:31–36 talk about when the Son of Man comes in His glory, with all His angels, and He takes His throne, all nations and people will be present. These Scriptures describe the dividing of the goats from His sheep. Our King Jesus will then remark to those gathered, "For I was hungry, and you fed me. I was thirsty, and you gave me a drink. I was a stranger, and you invited me into your home. I was naked, and you gave me clothing. I was sick, and you cared for me. I was in prison, and you visited me." Ministry we are called to, for and to our fellow humankind, is a CALLING into the prisons.

All Christians claiming to love Jesus are responsible for helping meet any person less fortunate and having needs. Only by the grace of our God we are not in some dire need ourselves. Jesus is always the answer, but He needs us and has called us to minister in His Name.

1. Have I ever considered youth detention or prison ministry?
2. If not, why not pray about these opportunities to

be the light in these dark areas?

3. If I do not go on a trip, maybe I am called to help finance those who go? Ask the Lord about this opportunity.

4. Spend some time in prayer and listen to God over these ministries.

Seed of Truth #45
(Kenya)

Becoming His Hand and Feet

Testimony by Kathie Stettler

Never did the words "be the hands and feet of Jesus" become so real as when I began to go on mission trips. It just never made sense to me what that meant.

After wanting to go on an international mission trip for many years, I was finally able to go in 2008. My daughter and I and seven others made a trip to Jamaica. There were so many unknowns and uncomfortable challenges. Raising the money for two individuals and traveling with a group of strangers, all for Jesus. Everything was a new experience.

Now I have always loved adventure and new opportunities, but this one seemed different, mainly because my 11-year-old was going along. Well, bottom line, I was hooked. My love for travel, coupled with helping others, no other experience fulfilled me like this trip.

What is memorable about a mission trip is that is changes who we are, probably more than the people to which we minister. One week away from your regular life allows for plenty of opportunities to realize how blessed we are to be Americans.

Interestingly, every trip offers new insight and revelation, a peeling away of "self" to uncover more gratitude and compassion for others. I made a promise to God to go on as many missions as He makes available to me. To date, this is my list: Guatemala (twice), Southeastern Europe (twice), Spain, and Kenya, and within the U.S.: Kentucky, Louisiana, and Georgia. What I see about mission trips is stepping out doesn't always mean into another country. There are plenty of opportunities close at hand. Going on these trips has helped me maintain a sense of balance in my own life. I appreciate the remarkable things and opportunities I have experienced, my husband's support, prayers shared for safety, so many lessons I could not have learned any other way.

Sometimes I return and get easily frustrated at Americans for not recognizing how great we live. Then I am reminded to have compassion for people who have not had the opportunity to see what I have witnessed. One of the most eye-opening experiences was in Kenya. An orphanage where the young ladies woke up at 5:30 am to sing, with their "angelic" voices to our Lord. Oh, how I miss waking up to these young voices singing praises. We don't do this here.

I brought art supplies and explained how to make vision boards. Here is a picture of what one young girl created. It still brings tears to my eyes to recognize we all have dreams and aspirations. Life has offered such a reward, so much more than I could ever have hoped for in traveling. I am showing people around the globe that Jesus loves us all.

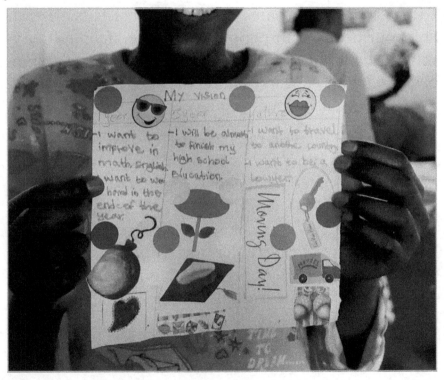

We are all made in His image and likeness. No matter our skin color, the language we speak, the different food we eat, or how we worship God, each of us is unique and memorable; the differences are only external.

A smile and touch are universal. Don't let fear hold you back from your purpose and exploring what is out there.

When God calls us, He equips us with the tools and people to assist. Life is a journey to be spent with our sisters and brothers in faith. I trust that 2021 will offer another opportunity to go somewhere, unsure when but I am ready, are you?

Peggy: This devotion is by a special prayer partner and friend of mine, Kathie Stettler. God brought us together to experience a mission trip several years ago. To date, we have shared three missions. Missions can knit your hearts with people and create lifetime friendships. I am so thankful to have her in my life. Remember, we are all beggars sharing the Bread of Life, Jesus, to other beggars in our world.

1. What is holding me back from answering the call of God on my life to be on mission for Jesus?
2. Am I too tied to the conveniences of my world to explore God's world?
3. Am I fearful and lacking trust to step out and find out the call He has on my life?
4. "Lord, this is my prayer. Open my heart to the people of your world who need Jesus, help me hear from You."

Seed of Truth #46
(Cairo, Egypt)

Life in the Dump

In 2005, a team from our church went to Cairo, Egypt. West Ridge had some connections there, so we had a variety of ministry planned. We would visit some of the Coptic Churches, schools, build some relationships, and hand out Christmas boxes to children supplied by Samaritan's Purse.

We attended some huge churches and spent time

building some relationships. I am still in contact with several of them via Facebook and Twitter. Our team's rooms at our hotel overlooked the Nile River. I never imagined I would lay eyes on the Nile River, a sight to behold. On our free night, we even got to take a boat ride on the river. Brace yourself; if you jump in God's Grace River, there is no telling what sights you might see in your lifetime.

Our team visited a beautiful enormous church built in a mountain. The steps leading down to the floor stage and altar area were deep into the mountain. This church seated thousands of people. It must have been a pretty picture when it was full of people. We were there when there was no service but it was a beautiful structure to behold.

The church building is located inside the perimeter of a garbage dump. As far as your eye can see, trash is mounded to the right and left of the opening area leading down into the church. Our host informed us that most of the people living in homes in and on the garbage dump were Christians. These churches were of Orthodox origin. Many of these Christians in this dump have garbage pick-up customers, which is how they make a living.

The children all gathered to greet us right next to a pigpen filled with baby and mama pigs. Our team would hand out the Christmas boxes from Samaritan's Purse to the children living in this area. I am a country girl; we had cows, pigs, and chickens, etc. I remember the smells we endured as children playing and working around the barn. Before exiting our bus, when we arrived, we prayed to God to help us not be overcome with the smells we were about to encounter. Several team members stayed on the bus to pray for us, who felt God calling us to get off and minister. I can honestly say, and others of the team would tell you, we smelled nothing that upset us. These little children gathering around us, by the pigpen, had flies on them, runny noses, and the stench was all around them and us. God had worked a miracle for the team. As God kept the smell of smoke off Daniel in the lion's den, He had kept these unpleasant smells from us. He is such a miracle-working God.

There are other miracles taking place in Egypt. We had numerous testimonies from the locals of how God gave visions to people who had no relationship with Him at all. People in some villages were all having the same dream during the same night. These visions or dreams would lead them to accept Jesus Christ as Savior. A few even shared God gave them a specific personal vision, and then they would meet the person of their dream, and they would lead them to Jesus as their Savior.

Along with the miracles God did for our team, we were privileged to see the pyramids. These, I must say, are a miracle to behold. The God of Egypt is the same God I love and serve here in the U.S. of America.

1. Do I believe that God can give visions and dreams to His children here in the States?
2. Have I ever experienced a dream or vision that I felt God was trying to tell me something? Am I open and eager for Him to speak with me these ways?
3. "Lord, prepare my mind, heart, and spirit to hear from You."

"A Time for Every Season!"

In the last four years, I have slowed down my international traveling. Somewhat because of my choice but primarily due to other reasons. One of the main reasons is my husband's health. In December 2016, he received a prostate cancer diagnosis. In our following five years, we dealt with operations and treatments.

The first year after surgery, we chose holistic care,

with an integrated doctor going the health route. After that first year and second surgery and some intense blood-cleansing treatments, cancer still moved to two more bones. In the fall of 2019, a new bone scan showed at least six bones metastasized with cancer. The urologists urged Don to begin a bone supplement and a hormone blocker as soon as possible. Much to our sadness, though, we learned his prostate-specific antigen (a protein that often indicates cancer) has risen higher because the medications did not work.

After meeting with our urologist, he recommended a new bone and computed tomography scan and an oncologist appointment. The results were staggering, with cancer spreading to at least ten new bones. Before radiation and chemo, Don's next decision was to take an adrenal gland blocker along with prednisone. The side effects of these drugs were not encouraging, but this was Don's choice. These drugs only lasted a few months before his numbers went up again.

In the middle of February 2021, Don had five radiation treatments to help with the pain in his left hip and down his leg. Jordan, our grandson's wedding was scheduled for the end of March 2021. Don wanted to be able to attend their wedding in Jamaica.

Considering Don's health stage, chemo was the next choice. He had a port put in on March 2 and he received a one-half dose of chemotherapy on March 4. All went well until the port got seriously infected a week later. He went into the hospital on March 17. He had to have the port removed on March 18. They gave him strong antibiotics to cure the infection. He came home on March 22, continuing the strong antibiotic.

We were able to attend Jordan and Carlee's wedding. We left on March 25 and returned home on March 30. We were so blessed to participate in their wedding and have a few extra days stay as well to relax.

The oncologist said Don would have the probability of at least six to eight full chemo treatments. The side effects from the first one-half chemo treatment had been minimal, excluding the port issue. He would, however, also have to have another port inserted to receive his subsequent chemo treatments.

We are many dollars shorter in our retirement account due to the problem health insurance does not cover integrated and holistic care. Which I might say, is ridiculous. But, as the saying goes, "You can't take it with you." It is just money. We continue to trust Don's health and our finances into God's hands; He carries us well, and He has supplied all our needs thus far. He will continue to give us wisdom in all our decisions. It is just sad because of all the insurance money we pay seems they do not really want you to be well!

After much prayer, thoughts, discussion, and soul-searching time, Don has decided he doesn't want another port or any chemo treatments. With much love and respect, I support his decision. He would like to enjoy the time he has left without medical intervention which brings the certainty of side effects and debilitating symptoms. He desires to be on the Lord's timetable and entrusts himself to Him. We are in His Sovereign hands.

In Our Season of Time

As I am writing this devotional book, we have experienced significant issues in our country for the past year and to date. The U.S., along with the world, is experiencing a health pandemic. We have been fighting a silent killer the authorities have titled COVID-19. It is a virus that originated in China but spread quickly throughout the world. Over two hundred thousand people have died from Covid19 related sicknesses in the U.S. Some are still becoming infected and treated. International flights are limited, and no trips are being made for mission work at this time by our Church or many other churches. A lot of borders are still closed at this time.

The virus began at the end of 2019. When our West Ridge team was in the United Kingdom on a mission in January of 2020, we started hearing about it on the news. We had our week of ministry and headed home through Italy. We spent a short layover in Italy and did some sightseeing. Flights were canceled in and out of the country shortly after we returned home. Italy became one of the areas to have the largest outbreak of the virus. God had faithfully protected our team and our health. Even though some of our group experienced a few health issues, we don't believe it was COVID-19.

Also, at the time of this writing, our country is divided over elected officials, especially for President's office. I served at the polls during our election. It has been the most voted election ever in our country. My heart breaks over all these issues. I woke up the day after the election, and my first words to God were, "Who won the election?" And, in the stillness of my spirit, I heard Him speak to me, "I did; I always win!" So, I am trying to continue in peace as our country is still in turmoil over many issues. What issues are you dealing with in your world?

What happens when kinks get thrown into your life plans? A sudden death, a job loss, a broken relationship, a severe health crisis, we never know what tomorrow holds. Most of us have never experienced anything like this pandemic or election issues.

One of my closest missionary friends was hospitalized for three months with COVID-19 and other complications. God miraculously brought him home on December 29, 2020. He is showing good signs of improvement as we continue to pray for his complete healing.

Even though I slowed down my traveling to ensure Don is getting the best care, the ministry of being on mission does not cease. God continues in my daily life to bring assignments to my door. Praying for the lost, praying for those who need healing, or sharing a cup of coffee with a friend who may need a listening ear. There are always opportunities at hand and in your community to be on mission for Jesus. God has been faithful during these last days, and we know He will continue to be whatever comes our way.

1. What is my response when God allows a kink in my schedule or untimely happenings in my life? Do I grow stronger or whine and complain?
2. Does my faith increase and grow more substantial when I hit troubled times?
3. Do I believe God ordains ALL of my steps? Man plans his ways, but the Word says, God is Sovereign and ordains my steps.

While You Are on
Mission Location

You are in a new culture in an international setting. One of the most damaging behaviors to indulge in is to insult a local. By this, an example would be if you needed to go to the bathroom and it is not clean and smelly, your negative response, if observed by a national, could either enhance or ruin your witness right off the bat. Remember, you are the example of Christ; you have come to share Christ, His ways, His acceptance, and His love with these people. If you begin to talk about the inconveniences, smells, or different lifestyle situations, you could lose them even before you have your first time to share Jesus with them. If you show any displeasure or discomfort due to their society, homes, foods, or personal appearance, you will have tarnished your testimony in front of them. Keep your comments to yourself if there is any possibility a local could overhear your remarks. You are not coming to change their culture but give them Jesus, and He will make the necessary changes for their welfare and culture. He will lead them to make needed life changes. You did not come to them as their Savior; you came to share your Savior with them.

Leaving There and Coming Home

I often make the statement that I leave a piece of my heart everywhere I go for the Lord. My heart must be very little now. You have seen many new things, experienced a different culture, and met locals who live very different from you and your family. Hopefully, your unique experiences, new friendships are tucked within your heart; and, you have an enlightened passion for the Lord because you served His people and creation. You are a part of the giant knitted canvas tapestry God is creating. You may only see the back of the tapestry at this time, with its knots, strings, different colors, none of them making a pretty sight. BUT GOD, He is the One creating the Masterpiece. What an honor you have experienced to be used in His Kingdom work. Someday you will know how you affected their lives. It would be best if you remembered a few things as you return home, back to your everyday life; your outlook on life has probably changed. Not your visual image but the spiritual eyes of your soul that captured every detail of your trip. You may experience some depression, even some righteous anger over the differences you have at home compared to your visited unprivileged location. You might find yourself not wasting food or taking an extra-long shower ever again. Trust me, you will go home different, and you will see things differently.

Don't get morbid or down in the dumps about these differences or feelings. Living in a country with God's blessings upon it should make you thankful and mindful to continue trying to bring healing to the world's impoverished places. These places may be in your back-yard or down the street or your inner city. God will use you wherever you are IF you keep your heart and spiritual ears open to Him.

You will try to share with your family and other people what you saw and experienced. Don't get upset with them when they don't understand or embrace the change in you. REMEMBER the saying, "You just had to be there!" BUT I recommend you DO NOT say that to them. Making that remark might offend them; they may think you are saying you are privileged or superior and, somehow, they are not. The treasures of service you hide in your heart from your trip will open new worlds to you; others will have to go and find their treasured memories. Continue to give God all the glory for what He accomplished through you and the team.

"Then the seventy returned with joy, saying, 'Lord, even the demons are subject to us in Your name.' And He said to them, 'I saw Satan fall like lightning from heaven. Behold, I give you the authority to trample on serpents and scorpions, and over all the power of the enemy, and nothing shall by any means hurt you. Nevertheless, do not rejoice in this, that the spirits are subject to you, but rather rejoice because your names are written in heaven."

Luke 10:17-20

Conclusion

I have so many other memories I could share but it is time to close. Over the last forty years, God has given me many unique invitations and opportunities to see His kingdom and His creation. In the coming months, my traveling will probably be limited, so I am now trying to be useful through ministry here in the States. The Covid19 pandemic has closed borders and made travel a lot more difficult for all international missionaries. Our church had to cancel every trip scheduled for the year 2020, and trips in the spring of 2021 continuing are debatable.

God is still working His miracles. Most churches, including ours, have not been able to hold services with people present in their buildings since March of 2020. Church services have been online, and this is how the shepherds (pastors) have been tending their flock with ministry from afar, encouragement, and messages online. Even though, now with limited numbers personally meeting within our church walls, we have continued to do ministry. We have provided food for the hungry, financial help to those desperately in need of losing their homes, money to pay overdue bills due to job loss, so many hurting people our church has reached out to serve through kingdom work. Our online services have reached people we would never have connected with without this pandemic. God has a way to work His plans, even in troubled times, and He uses His children and His church and every available resource because He LOVES.

Our prison team has not been able to go into prison for ministry since March 2020 as well. The team leaders have arranged prayer times and teaching times, so we on the outside could stay encouraged and hopeful for a day soon to return behind bars for ministry. My prayer has been that the same BIG, FAITHFUL, SOVEREIGN GOD has shown up to my incarcerated sisters, and they are standing firm in their faith in the Lord Jesus.

Our country has unrest and turmoil due to the Presidential election, health pandemic, heightened stress, racist restlessness, financial breakdowns, loss of jobs, and businesses closing. I trust that God's timing for this book will be an encouragement to you and the CALLING He has placed on your life, starting at home first, then community, and the world.

"Then I heard the Lord asking, 'Whom should I send as a messenger to this people?' I said, here I am. Send me." Isaiah 6:8

"I have come to see clearly that life is more than self. It is more than doing what I want, striving for what will benefit me, dreaming of all I can be. Life is all about my relationship with God. There is no higher CALLING, no loftier dream, and no greater goal than to live, breathe, and be poured out for Jesus Christ." (Jamie in Brother Andrew's "The Calling" Brother Andrew, The Narrow Road: Stories of Those Who Walk This Road Together (With this Road CD by Jars of Clay).

Will you answer His CALL on your life?

About The Author

Peggy W. Lester

Peggy was ordained under Faith Christian Fellowship International in Eaton, Ohio. She is a short-term Christian missionary, speaker, and teacher. She received a bachelor's degree in Christian Counseling and is a 2009 graduate of "She Speaks," a Proverbs 31 Ministry based in North Carolina.

Peggy's heart was *captured for missions* by the Lord in 1980. Since then, she has traveled locally and abroad, speaking about the Lord and being His disciple. She uses humor, boldness, and the Word of God to share the message of Christ. Peggy believes, "we are all ministers of the Gospel; some can travel far, all should serve near, and all can pray and share their resources."

Peggy and her husband, Don, have ministered to

young adults and singles for many years. Mentoring young couples is very dear to her heart. She believes in "the family" and that it is the essential organism next to the Church of Jesus Christ. She has spoken often about family dynamics, raising children, marriage, and passing a Godly heritage to the next generation. She has accumulated many hours of counseling with marriages in crisis on the mission field and at home.

Peggy's newest opportunity is to women behind bars. She is part of a team that goes in monthly to a maximum women's prison to do ministry. Also, she takes part in a weekend, twice a year, where there are 30 to 36 inmates ministered to for a full weekend beginning on Thursday evening. Scripture says, when you minister to the incarcerated, you are ministering to Jesus. It is an enriching and much-needed ministry.

Peggy will touch your heart, sharing her personal story, as well as her international travels and local missions. Wherever she goes, she desires to carry the "fragrance of Christ" and share passionately about her love for the Lord and His love for all people. She has a 501(c)(3) non-profit organization called Spreading His Fragrance Near and Far, Inc., founded in 2010.

Peggy and Don, her husband of over 54 years, have two married sons, two daughter-in-loves, five grandchildren, and one great-grandson. They currently reside West of Atlanta, Georgia.

When Peggy is not traveling or ministering, she enjoys spending time with family.

P.O. Box 453
Powder Springs, Georgia 30127
www.entegritypublishing.com
info@entegritypublishing.com
770.727.6517

CPSIA information can be obtained
at www.ICGtesting.com
Printed in the USA
LVHW021242181121
703694LV00012B/824